Taxation of International Portfolio Investment

Taxation of International Portfolio Investment

by

Donald J.S. Brean
Richard M. Bird
and
Melvyn Krauss

Centre for Trade Policy and Law
and
The Institute for Research on Public Policy
L'Institut de recherches politiques

336.2
B828t

Printed in Canada

Legal Deposit Second Quarter
Bibliothèque nationale du Québec

Canadian Cataloguing in Publication Data

Brean, Donald J.S., date.

Taxation of international portfolio investment

Prefatory material in English and French.
Includes bibliographical references.

ISBN 0-88645-123-X

1. Investments, Foreign—Taxation. 2. Taxation,
Double. 3. Taxation—Canada. I. Bird, Richard
M., 1938- II. Krauss, Melvyn B. III. Centre for
Trade Policy and Law. IV. Institute for Research on
Public Policy. V. Title.

HJ2341.B73 1991   336.2   C91-097595-7

Camera-ready copy and publication management by
PDS Research Publishing Services Ltd.
P.O. Box 3296
Halifax, Nova Scotia B3J 3H7

Published by
The Centre for Trade Policy and Law
Room 204, Social Sciences Research Building
Carleton University
Ottawa, Ontario K1S 5B6
and
The Institute for Research on Public Policy
P.O. Box 3670 South
Halifax, Nova Scotia B3J 3K6

Contents

List of Tables and Figures

Tables

Figures

Foreword

"Globalization" has entered the popular lexicon with a far broader meaning than the traditional concepts of economic interdependence. Today terms such as "the borderless economy" are used to describe the growing interpenetration of national economies arising from the growing mobility of portfolio capital, direct investment, technology and human capital in conjunction with expansion of information flows and services trade.

This study by Donald Brean, Richard Bird and Melvyn Krauss examines the implications for tax policy of the growing mobility of portfolio capital. Portfolio capital flows have grown much more rapidly than direct investment flows which, in turn, have grown more rapidly than international trade flows. The policy issues examined are of relevance to both creditor economies and debtor economies. Nonetheless the issues are of particular relevance to the Canadian economy because Canada has a substantial dependence upon portfolio capital inflows and has accumulated substantial liabilities in recent decades. Canada presently has net foreign liabilities of $250 billion, much larger on a per capita basis than is the case for any other industrialized nation. As the preface by the authors indicates, this manuscript, which started as an examination of some specialized questions in international tax policy, has evolved into a discussion of a much broader set of issues. The topics examined have become more relevant to an understanding of the pressures acting upon domestic tax systems and national tax policies as well as arcane international arrangements.

In particular, when financial and human capital are highly mobile, the viability of both the corporate and the personal income tax systems of individual countries can be eroded. In the face of growing economic interdependence, the scope for effective exercise of sovereign powers in shaping national tax policies will be largely determined by the international context discussed in this study. The Institute and the Centre for Trade Policy and Law are pleased to be able to contribute this analysis to the broadening debate over the place of nation-states in an integrated global marketplace.

Rod Dobell   Murray G. Smith
President   Director
Institute for Research   Centre for Trade
on Public Policy   Policy and Law

April 1991

Avant-propos

En entrant dans le lexique populaire, le mot globalisation a pris un sens beaucoup plus large que celui d'interdépendance économique auquel le confinait la langue économique traditionnelle. De nos jours, des expressions comme économie sans frontières servent à décrire l'interpénétration de plus en plus grande des économies nationales qui découle de la mobilité croissante des capitaux en portefeuille, des investissements directs, de la technologie et des ressources humaines, mobilité qui va de conserve avec l'expansion du flot de l'information et celle du commerce des services.

Cette étude, que l'on doit à Donald Brean, Richard Bird et Melvyn Krauss, a pour propos d'examiner les implications qu'entraîne la mobilité croissante du capital en portefeuille sur la politique fiscale. Les capitaux en valeurs mobilières se sont en effet accrus beaucoup plus rapidement que ceux consacrés aux investissements directs, lesquels ont, à leur tour, augmenté à un rythme plus grand que celui des échanges commerciaux internationaux. Les problèmes de politique générale qui sont étudiés ici concernent aussi bien les économies créditrices que débitrices. Toutefois, ces questions sont aussi d'une importance particulière pour le Canada parce que ce pays dépend considérablement des entrées en capitaux de portefeuille et parce qu'il a accumulé, au cours des dernières décennies, un passif considérable. À l'heure actuelle, le Canada affiche, à l'égard de l'étranger, un passif de l'ordre de 250 milliards de dollars, ce qui représente un montant par habitant beaucoup plus important que pour n'importe quel autre pays industrialisé. Comme l'indique la préface rédigée par ces auteurs, leur analyse, qui visait initialement à préciser certains aspects spécifiques de politique fiscale internationale, a tout naturellement abouti à l'examen critique d'un ensemble de questions beaucoup plus vaste. Cela devenait nécessaire si l'on voulait comprendre les pressions auxquelles sont soumis les systèmes fiscaux domestiques et les politiques fiscales nationales, et déchiffrer les arcanes des ententes internationales.

Lorsque les ressources financières et humaines s'avèrent être d'une grande mobilité, l'intégrité des systèmes d'imposition sur le revenu des corporations et des particuliers d'un pays donné peut être remise en question. Étant donné la croissance continue de l'interdépendance économique, la marge de manoeuvre effective dont pourront disposer les pouvoirs souverains dans l'élaboration des politiques fiscales nationales sera, en grande partie, fonction du contexte international dont il est question dans cette étude. L'Institut et le Centre de droit et de politique commerciale sont heureux de pouvoir ajouter cette analyse au débat sans cesse grandissant qui porte sur le rôle des États-nations au sein d'une économie de marché globale.

Rod Dobell
Président
L'Institut de recherches
politiques

Murray G. Smith
Directeur
Centre de droit et
de politique commerciale

Avril 1991

Preface

This study has had a convoluted history. It began several years ago as a shorter and rather different paper by Krauss and Bird discussing several aspects of fiscal interdependence in an increasingly integrated world economy. Subsequently, it was substantially revised and expanded by Brean and re-oriented to focus more specifically on the taxation of international portfolio investment. The present version incorporates still further revisions by Brean and Bird, as well as the helpful—if not always consistent—comments of what seems to have been an endless series of reviewers over the years. Throughout this lengthy process, the various research directors of the Institute for Research on Public Policy who have grappled with the succeeding versions of the paper have been remarkably patient.

   The final results as presented here thus incorporate aspects of the work of three different authors working at different times and, for the most part, in geographically separate locales. The fact that this paper is neither a complete nor a fully integrated treatment of its subject, however, is more a reflection of the extreme complexity of the international taxation issue than of the circumstances of its origin. Basically, four separate issues are discussed in this study:

(1) the "simple analytics" of taxing international capital income flows (Chapters 2 and 3); (2) the national and international institutional arrangements for such taxation (Chapters 4 to 6); (3) some aspects of the complex relation between taxation, inflation, exchange rates, and international capital flows (Chapters 7 and 8); and (4) the implications of all this for Canada—a subject which is touched on at various places throughout the study as well as in Chapter 9. The aim is more to provide a flavour of the issues and the sort of analysis that is possible in the absence of much empirical data than to provide definitive answers to the complex questions arising in this field. There can be few more important areas for research and thought in the public area than international taxation. Despite the preliminary state of the results presented here, perhaps those who work through this material—which, while highly simplified is, in the nature of the subject, by no means simple—will end up both with a better grasp of what is at stake with respect to international taxation and with the determination to improve on what we have been able to do.

Donald J.S. Brean
Richard M. Bird
Melvyn Krauss

Donald J.S. Brean is Associate Professor of Finance and Economics in the Faculty of Management, University of Toronto. While preparing this monograph he was Visiting Scholar in the Faculty of Economics and Politics, Cambridge University, England.

Richard M. Bird is Professor of Economics at the University of Toronto. While completing this monograph he was Tinbergen Visiting Professor of Economics at Erasmus University, Rotterdam, The Netherlands.

Melvyn Krauss is Professor of Economics at New York University and Senior Fellow of the Hoover Institute at Stanford University, Palo Alto, California.

1.

Introduction

International economic integration is steadily changing the structure of national economies as well as the policies that nations can realistically pursue. On the one hand sovereign nations realize that their economic growth and industrial development depend crucially on world markets. Such growth and development generally requires freer trade and fewer restrictions on the international flow of factors of production—capital, labour, and technology. On the other hand, open economies are constrained in terms of the national policies that they can adopt in their own self-interest. Protectionist trade policies in particular tend to make small open economies worse off.

International economic integration has come to mean much more than expanded trade. International *direct* investment—the stuff of multinational enterprise—is surpassing trade as the principal vehicle for international commerce. Direct investment is often a more effective way of penetrating foreign markets and serving offshore customers. The recent U.S.-Canada Free Trade Agreement and the current GATT round address the liberalization of international investment as well as trade.

The vast bulk of international capital flows, however, does not involve direct investment in specific offshore plants and operations. Rather, the greatest volume of international finance consists of commercial and government borrowing in international capital markets. Canadian participation in offshore lending and borrowing, for example, has grown by more than 30 percent per year throughout the 1980s. The volume of new debt transactions exceeds direct investment by a factor of 10. The growth of cross-border exchange of outstanding Canadian securities is even more spectacular—about 200 percent per year throughout the '80s. Indeed, the unprecedented development of global capital markets reflects a world awash with stateless capital that flows rapidly to sites of highest return.

In contrast to the theory of trade, international capital gives rise to more complex analytic problems and policy prescriptions. Furthermore, the effects of alternative national policies are less certain in world in which *both* goods and capital are internationally mobile. The estimated effects of policy invariably depend on assumptions concerning the economics of foreign investment. Taxation in particular has an international policy dimension that seems to be at least a step behind real developments in the rapidly integrating world economy.

In principle, the international dimension of tax policy falls within the purview of both public finance and international economics. Unfortunately, both sides have been somewhat remiss in dealing with this area. Public finance analyses for the most part focus on fiscal operations in a closed economy with no regard for international trade or factor flows. Models of international trade, on the other hand, assume a world in which the tariff is the major policy instrument. Such approaches tend either to ignore the passive reality of government or else to treat it in a relatively superficial and artificial way (see Dixit, 1985).

The real world is characterized by trade and factor flows and governments that intervene in various ways. To understand this world better, it is important to merge the literature of public finance with that of international economics to illuminate the economic problems that result from the international interaction of national policies. This should provide rules to guide policy in an interdependent world.

This monograph provides a brief, schematic outline of the economics of international capital with special attention to the role of taxation in determining the size and division of the economic gain from foreign investment. The analysis focuses primarily on *portfolio* capital, defined as international investment in the form of debt and, to a lesser extent, non-controlling equity.

Portfolio capital is not imported in crates. It flows primarily through the international bond markets. Since portfolio investors are interested in the rate of return on the securities they hold, the most important factors determining the direction and volume of portfolio capital are international interest differentials. Taxes affect portfolio investment flows through their effects on after-tax financial yields.

We take a Canadian perspective on these international issues. At the present time Canada has a substantial net financial debt, approximately $230 billion, to the rest of the world. Canada has international assets of $80 billion and international liabilities of $310 billion. More than 60 percent of Canada's net indebtedness is portfolio capital consisting of Canadian government and corporate bonds held by foreigners less the value of foreign bonds owned by Canadians. The net interest and dividends paid by Canada to the rest of the world exceed $22 billion annually (1989).

Historically, Canadian investments abroad have been predominantly in portfolio capital while investment by foreigners in Canada has been heavily in direct investment. This is changing. Canadian outward investment is increasingly direct while the much larger volume of Canadian inward investment is increasingly portfolio. In 1970 the ratio of portfolio to direct investment that foreigners had in Canada was approximately 3:5. By 1988 the ratio had reversed to approximately 5:3. Obviously foreign investors are increasing their purchases of Canadian bonds more rapidly than their purchases of Canadian subsidiaries.

Demographic, technological, and fiscal factors—in particular the rapid growth of the Canadian labour force, the relative capital-intensity of Canada's fastest growing industries, and the public sector deficits of recent years—all add to a demand for investment in Canada which, to the extent that the demand exceeds domestic savings, is met through foreign capital inflows. On the other hand, whenever Canadian savings exceed domestic needs, Canadian capital flows abroad—through banks, insurance companies and the like—to fill financial gaps in other nations.

Outline

A convenient starting point to deal with the economics of international portfolio capital is to consider equilibrium in international financial flows, as we do in the next chapter. If Canada were unable to attract sufficient foreign capital to meet its needs, or if international capital flows were otherwise inhibited, the value of a unit of capital in Canada (the value of the marginal unit of output produced by capital in Canada) would be higher than elsewhere, a direct reflection of Canada's capital shortage. This state of disequilibrium cannot persist for long in an integrated world capital market. Our first model explains the international capital realignment toward equilibrium effected through international portfolio capital movements. The model incorporates taxation and offers a convenient framework for exploring more complicated issues that will arise later.

The degree of international capital market integration is an institutional issue that is crucial to analysis of international tax questions. We assume a high degree of integration subject to to certain restrictions—such as taxation—that inhibit or divert the otherwise free flow of capital. The economic role of international capital markets that are transactionally and informationally efficient is not so much a matter of convenient assumption as it is recognition of a facet of modern reality. Overwhelming evidence points to the fact that portfolio capital—involving mobile, fungible, easily transported and storable financial assets—is traded and valued in highly competitive and efficient markets. International capital markets maintain an integrated set of real interest rates and costs of capital across countries. This is not to say, however, that the international ebb and flow of portfolio capital has an immediate and direct counterpart in the allocation of productive physical capital, an important point to receive more attention later.

Following the discussion of taxation and the international allocation of capital in Chapter 2, Chapter 3 extends the analysis to show the symmetry of taxes on trade and taxes on foreign investment. This parallel is convenient for policy analysis, especially insofar as there is more general familiarity with the international trade model and the issues it addresses.

Chapter 4 explores the nebulous concept of neutrality as this criterion is used to identify economic distortions or to govern policy with respect to international capital flows. Neutrality, as typically invoked, is a criterion for efficiency from the world perspective; the means to achieve neutrality have implications for the international distribution of the benefits of foreign investment. The point is important since policy in most countries is driven more by nationalist distributional considerations than by concern for efficient international allocation of capital. Chapter 4 also outlines the nature of the tax arrangements that are required to attain neutrality when, as is commonly the case, countries have different systems of corporate and personal income taxes.

Chapter 5 presents an overview of the principal institutional mechanism, the tax treaty, used to resolve conflict inherent in bilateral tax issues. Chapter 6 looks in some detail at Canadian tax policy with respect to foreign-source earnings. Chapter 7 discusses a striking example of a perverse international interaction—an arrangement that potentially drives capital from a country with relatively higher returns to a country with lower returns.

Chapter 8 analyses the international dimension of a long-standing problem in the taxation of capital—the effects of taxing nominal rather than real capital income. When more than one country is involved, the issue entails *relative* inflation rates, interest rates, and tax rates. We demonstrate that under reasonable assumptions of interest rate and exchange rate adjustments to inflation, taxation of nominal interest in both countries causes capital to flow to the country with relatively greater inflation. Chapter 9 is a summary and an outline of the implications for Canadian tax policy.

2.

Taxation and the International Allocation of Capital

International Efficient Allocation of Capital

Capital is efficiently allocated between two places—or between two uses—if the value of the marginal output of capital is equal in both places (or both uses). As a rule, internationally mobile capital flows from a country that offers relatively low marginal returns, reflecting a relative abundance of capital, to a country that offers relatively higher marginal returns associated with less capital relative to its labour and/or its productive opportunities. The international flow of capital is ultimately constrained by the fact that increases in the stock of capital in the capital-importing nation reduce the marginal return on capital. By the same token, the marginal return on capital in a capital-exporting country rises as a result of the outflow of capital.

Figure 2.1 graphically depicts the key relationships in a bilateral context. The horizontal axis represents the total stock of capital in two representative countries, Home and Foreign. Reading from the left of the axis, O_h is the origin of for Home. The capital stock of Foreign is read from right to left with origin O_f. The solid downward sloping lines from the left and right vertical axes, hh and ff, represent pre-tax marginal returns on capital at

7

Home and in Foreign respectively. The negative slopes of these lines reflect diminishing marginal returns on investment. The broken lines, h'h' and f'f', are after-tax returns on capital. The ratio hh'/hO_h is the proportional tax rate imposed by Home while ff'/fO_f is the tax rate imposed by Foreign.

The point K denotes the initial allocation of capital. O_hK is in Home, KO_f is in Foreign. With this allocation the marginal return on investment in Home (at w) exceeds the marginal return in Foreign (at y). The differential (w – y) reflects an inefficient international allocation of capital and foregone capital income. Capital shifted from Foreign to Home results in expanded output of the two nations combined. A unit of capital shifted from Foreign to Home causes output in Foreign to decrease by y, output in Home to increase by w, and a net increase in output amounting to w – y.

In a world of perfectly mobile capital and no taxes, capital flows from Foreign to Home up to the point K*. K* depicts the efficient international allocation of capital, satisfying the criterion of equal pre-tax marginal returns. The mechanism for international capital reallocation from Foreign to Home, of course, is for Home to sell net financial assets (bonds) to Foreign.

Taxation of Interest on Foreign Capital

Interest is paid by bond issuers in the capital-importing nation, Home in the example, to bond holders in the capital-exporting nation, Foreign. If the interest paid on Home-bonds is subject to tax by either country, capital is then allocated efficiently only if the international structure of tax provides the private after-tax incentive for Foreign purchasers to hold exactly K-K* of Home bonds. In other words, international capital is efficiently allocated by market forces only if the *after-tax* equilibrium (at the intersection of h'h' and f'f') is identical to the *pre-tax* equilibrium (at the intersection of hh and ff).

In short, international *economic efficiency* is determined by the equality of the pre-tax marginal returns whereas international *financial equilibrium* is determined by the equality of after-tax marginal returns. Taxation may introduce "wedges" that distort the international allocation of capital. A tax wedge is created when *after-tax* returns are equated at an international capital allocation such that *pre-tax* returns are not equal. In the diagram, K^* is consistent with both international allocative efficiency and financial equilibrium through explicit construction. Any number of international tax structures could result in a market equilibrium that is not allocatively efficient.

Figure 2.1
The Simple Analytics of Foreign Investment:
Allocative Efficiency and the Distribution of Benefits

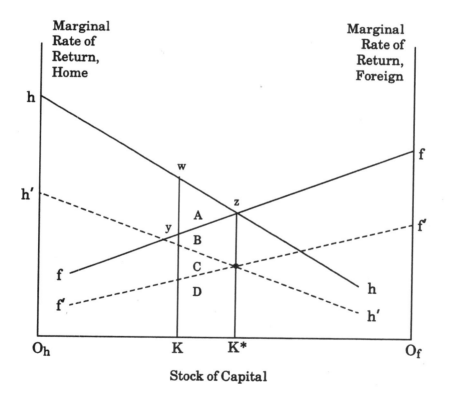

Stock of Capital

Areas A, B, C and D in Figure 2.1 illustrate the productive and distributive consequences of the international reallocation of capital from the inefficient allocation at K to the efficient allocation at K^*. Triangle A represents the expanded income resulting from the more productive use of capital (K-K^*) shifted from Foreign to Home. Area C plus D represents after-tax income from the additional capital in Home owned by investors residing in Foreign. Area C alone is the increase in global after-tax income— that is, the private share of the efficiency gains. Area D also involves an increase in foreign-source income. However, since D is identical to the reduction in domestic source after-tax income in Foreign, it does not represent a global expansion of private income.

Areas A and B represent tax flows. However, it is not clear which national treasury receives—or which is entitled to receive— the tax revenue. It could be the country of the source of income, Home, or the investor's country of residence, Foreign. Indeed, for purposes of international allocative efficiency it does not matter whether the priority claim to tax rests with the capital-exporting country or the capital-importing country. That is a distributive issue. Efficient international allocation of capital is consistent with any international distribution of the tax revenue, A plus B.

Allocative Efficiency and Financial Equilibrium

Private investors allocate capital efficiently as long as the effective tax on the bonds issued by Home is equal to the rate in effect in the capital-exporting country, Foreign. In terms of Figure 2.1, the private investors' objective is to realize triangle C. If private investors in Foreign are taxed at a rate other than the rate implicit in the slope of ff'—that is, other than the domestic tax rate in Foreign—international allocation of capital through private investment decisions will not yield triangles A and C. Efficiency thus requires the earnings of foreign-owned capital to be taxed at the effective tax rate levied in the country of residence. This international allocative rule of taxation is termed "capital export neutrality". In essence, capital export neutrality requires that international investors—the purveyors of mobile capital—be indifferent between domestic and foreign investment on a *pre-tax* as well as on an after-tax basis.

There are three alternative methods to ensure that foreign-source earnings are taxed at the appropriate rate to achieve capital export neutrality. First, the source country may tax imported capital at a variety of rates based on the country of origin of the imported capital, while residence countries do not tax at all.

Second, the source country may refrain from taxing the earnings of foreign capital, leaving such income to be taxed only by residence (capital-exporting) countries. Finally, the source country may tax the income of foreign capital while the residence country also taxes such income but provides full credit for foreign taxes paid. While each of these arrangements would in principle result in capital export neutrality and international allocative efficiency, in practice some variant of the last, the foreign tax credit system, is the most common and the most relevant to Canada in its role both as capital importer and capital exporter.

Interpreting the Model in the Canadian Context

Canada employs a large stock of foreign-owned capital. As noted above, Canadian net financial indebtedness to the rest of the world today exceeds $230 billion, more than 60 percent of which is a net portfolio liability. $K - K^*$ in the model represents the accumulated net stock of foreign-owned capital in Canada—our net liability to the rest of the world. Historically, investment in Canada has offered higher yields to investors, both domestic and foreign investors, than comparable-risk investments elsewhere. The reasons are part of our economic heritage—new frontiers, an influx of immigrant labour, the need for infrastructure, the capital intensity of the resource industries—all of which created a need for capital which outstripped the domestic capacity to generate savings for investment. In light of the relative maturity in this sense of British and European economies, investors abroad found the Canadian need for capital provided an attractive alternative to domestic investment.

As set out above, the equilibrium foreign-owned capital stock in Canada is determined by the amount of capital needed to establish equality of the marginal return on all Canadian capital and the marginal return abroad. The market allocates capital within and among countries until no differential exists between either the after-tax marginal return on domestic and foreign-owned investment in Canada or between the after-tax marginal return on investment in Canada and investment elsewhere.

Capital Stocks and Flows

The distinction between capital *stock* and *flow* is crucial to this discussion of international capital market behaviour. The *stock* of capital is the total volume of capital in place that together with labour and other resources generate the nation's economic output. Other things, technology in particular, being equal, the marginal return on capital is determined by the stock of capital relative to the stock of the other factors of production. Our model demonstrates that disequilibrium is identified by differentials in marginal returns to capital; such differentials give rise to international reallocation of the national stocks of capital. A *change* in a stock of capital is defined as a *flow*. With respect to foreign capital movements in a particular period, such flows obviously may be positive or negative for a given country depending on its needs relative to the rest of the world. In fact, net flows of capital generally constitute a relatively small fraction of the accumulated net foreign-owned stock of capital. The annual net international flow of capital in or out of Canada is seldom more than five per cent of the total or cumulative net liability.

A state of international equilibrium in capital allocation is characterized by a random pattern of positive and negative net flows. On the other hand, a continuous net inflow or outflow of foreign capital reflects persistent external imbalance. Equilibrium is restored through a change in the stock of foreign capital— through expanded sales of financial assets to foreigners or net repurchases foreign held assets. Clearly, capital imports augment domestic savings while capital exports represent an overflow of domestic savings.

Changes in the equilibrium capital stock of an open economy —indicated by persistent external imbalance—result primarily from structural economic changes in that country or in the relative structure of that country and the rest of the world. For example, an increased demand for a capital-intensive output, such as Canadian mineral resources, would lead to an increase in the equilibrium stock of capital in Canada. With respect to the ownership of capital, if a nation's total capital requirement increases or if the domestic supply of savings falls, the ratio of foreign-to-domestic capital generally will rise.[2]

Capital Imports for Production or Consumption

To this point we have focussed on the international differential in the marginal returns in productive capital as the key economic factor underlying an international reallocation of capital. Indeed, most "textbook" approaches to portfolio investment identify the marginal return on capital as the determinant of the interest rate and disregard the marginal rate of time preference for consumption. The marginal rate of time preference for consumption is perhaps a more relevant factor in explanations of portfolio capital movements, at least in the shorter term. Explanations of why countries borrow to consume rather than to invest are consistent with the observations that increased foreign indebtedness does not necessarily give rise to corresponding increases in the productive capital base of the capital importing nation.

There are numerous macroeconomic reasons why foreign portfolio capital may flow into (or out of) a country without inducing a change in factor capital employed in domestic industry. For example, at a given level of domestic income, an increase in domestic consumption (and thus a reduction in domestic savings) requires an increased inflow of foreign capital—or a reduced outflow of domestic capital—merely to maintain the original level of investment. The foreign capital inflow thus finances increased domestic consumption or, alternatively, it augments domestic savings.

Public sector fiscal deficits in an open economy may be financed in part through growth of foreign indebtedness, again without necessarily expanding the domestic factor capital base. For example, when the government finances a fiscal deficit by issuing bonds that cannot be fully absorbed in domestic markets, some bonds must be sold to foreigners (directly or indirectly through a "crowding out" of the domestic bond market). Thus the expanded domestic spending within the fiscal deficit is to some extent financed with foreign capital. To complicate matters further, the expanded domestic spending will both reduce exports and increase imports. This is not incremental to the foreign finance of the deficit, but rather it takes another perspective: the accounting identities of the Balance of Payments require trade deficits (and surpluses) to have counterparts in foreign capital inflows and (outflows).

The various reasons why foreign portfolio capital may flow to one country from another illustrate that there is not a direct one-for-one linkage between changes in foreign financial capital and domestic factor capital. Nevertheless, to the extent that the domestic savings ratio is relatively constant, fiscal and trade imbalances are not chronic, and monetary reserves are not hoarded, the long-run growth in the stock of foreign capital relaxes the financial constraint on real investment (otherwise determined by domestic savings) and thus facilitates expansion of the stock of factor capital in the capital-importing nation.

The Capital Account of the Canadian Balance of Payments

Table 2.1 shows the recent pattern of international finance flowing through the Capital Account of the Canadian Balance of Payments. Inflows (positive entries) and outflows (negative entries) of both foreign direct and portfolio capital are reported along with net figures in the respective categories. The four columns on the right hand side of the table summarize the annual flows of net liabilities according to the major categories. It is clear that in recent years the substantial net inflow of long-term capital into Canada has been virtually all net portfolio capital. Indeed, Canada has been a net exporter of direct investment through the Balance of Payments every year since 1975, largely owing to the substantial volume of foreign direct investments by Canadians as opposed to a reduction in investment by the foreign sector in Canada, although nationalization of the petroleum sector and the economic slump of the early '80s did result in some such reduction. The continuous net *inflow* of portfolio capital throughout this period, however, suggests that Canada has less than its equilibrium stock of such capital in the sense that we are to the left of K^* in the model sketched above. One reason appears to have been a general upward shift of hh, the schedule of marginal returns on capital placed in Canada. Major increases in the rates of flow of portfolio capital into Canada occurred in the inflationary periods of 1973-76 and 1979-82. We shall have more to say about the interaction of inflation, taxation, and capital flows later.

Table 2.1
Canadian Balance of International Payments: Capital Account, Selected Statistics 1970 – 1989
(millions of dollars)

Year	Canadian Claims on Non-Residents, Net Flows				Canadian Liabilities to Non-Residents, Net Flows				Net Liabilities, Flows			
	Canadian Direct Invest Abroad	Foreign Portfolio Stocks	Foreign Portfolio Bonds	Long Term Portfolio Investment by Canada	Direct Investment in Canada	Canadian Stocks Held by Foreigners	Canadian Bonds Held by Foreigners	Long Term Portfolio Investment in Canada	Net Capital Movements	Net Direct Investment	Net Long Term Portfolio Flows	Net Short-Term Portfolio and Other
1989	-4900	-768	-1556	-2324	3400	3870	17069	20939	22070	-1500	18615	4955
1988	-7319	-1020	-74	-1094	4800	-2379	15870	13491	14200	-2519	12397	4322
1987	-8681	-1067	-874	-1941	4401	6641	7624	14265	12254	-4280	12324	4210
1986	-5650	-2065	-179	-2244	1375	1877	22541	24418	12729	-4275	22174	-5170
1985	-3900	-570	-750	-1320	-2800	1551	11066	12617	8209	-6700	11297	3612
1984	-2949	-714	-1359	-2073	1700	152	7708	7860	3742	-1249	5787	-796
1983	-3400	-825	-451	-1276	300	912	4780	5692	2626	-3100	4416	1310
1982	-875	-309	-234	-543	-1025	-309	11965	11656	-713	-1900	11113	-9926
1981	-6900	8	-31	-23	-4400	-629	11504	10875	14587	-11300	10852	15035
1980	-3150	-115	-68	-183	800	1490	3461	4951	2306	-2350	4768	-112
1979	-2550	-613	31	-583	750	523	3552	4075	7372	-1800	3493	5679
1978	-2325	75	-49	26	135	-270	5267	4997	8049	-2190	5023	5216
1977	-740	244	-21	223	475	-105	5280	5175	6546	-265	5398	1413
1976	-590	20	57	77	-300	-57	8636	8579	7876	-890	8656	110
1975	-915	42	-60	-18	725	87	4407	4494	5957	-190	4476	1671
1974	-810	67	-10	48	845	-139	1866	1727	2331	35	1775	521
1973	-770	118	-48	70	830	13	577	590	538	60	660	-182
1972	-400	272	-28	244	620	-24	1379	1355	1847	220	1599	28
1971	-230	221	-25	196	925	-125	233	108	919	695	304	-80
1970	-315	90	-20	70	905	-79	572	493	-717	590	563	-1870

Note: Canadian long-term bond obligations include those of the Government of Canada, federal government enterprises, provincial and municipal governments, and corporations. Short term portfolio and other flows through the Capital Account include changes in international reserves and loans and subscriptions of the Government of Canada, chartered banks' net foreign currency position with non-residents, money market investments, and the allocation of Special Drawing Rights.

Source: Bank of Canada Review, December 1990. Table J3: Canadian Balance of International Payments: Capital Account, with authors' computations of Net Liabilities, Flows.

Table 2.2 shows the stocks of Canada's foreign assets and liabilities and corresponding net positions for selected years from 1960 to 1988. Canada's stock of portfolio investment abroad has consistently been 10 to 20 percent of the size of the stock of foreign portfolio investment in Canada. Two important points of contrast arise between these stock statistics and the flow statistics discussed above.[3] First, the annual net long term portfolio flow is relatively small, generally less than 5 percent, when compared to the stock of national net indebtedness. Second, in terms of variability, the stock of total Canadian net indebtedness has risen rather steadily since 1970 whereas, as one would expect, the flows have much greater year-to-year variance.

Figure 2.2 presents a graphic summary of the relatively recent changes in the stock composition of the Canadian International Investment Position. In terms of assets, that is "Canadian capital abroad", Canadians have substantially increased the share in the form of direct investment. That investment, currently more than 75 percent of the total, ranges from Alcan's offshore aluminum operations to the Zale chain recently acquired by Peoples Jewellers. Canadian capital, technology and business acumen is directly exported by firms as diverse as McCains, Bombardier, Northern Telecom, and Olympia and York.

On the asset side, Canada is unique among industrialized nations in terms of the increase in the ratio of direct to portfolio investment. The relative volume and growth of outward direct investment to some extent reflects the successful pursuit of foreign markets and specific offshore production opportunities for Canadian firms. On the other hand, the decline in the relative share of portfolio investment in Canadian assets reflects the fact that domestic *Canadian* financial issues are attractive to Canadian investors. Canadian interest rates have remained sufficiently high to have Canadian opt for Canadian as opposed to foreign bonds. The underlying macroeconomic reasons for this are discussed at greater length in next chapter.

On the liabilities side, the same high relatively Canadian interest rates that are keeping domestic savings at home are also attracting foreign savings. At the same time, direct investment in Canada by foreigners has moderated for several reasons, most of which relate more to the changing structure of international

Table 2.2
Canada's Balance of Foreign Direct and Portfolio Investment, Selected Year-ends, 1960 – 1988
(billions of dollars)

	1988	1986	1984	1982	1980	1978	1976	1970	1965	1960
Canadian Assets										
Direct Investment	61.2	53.2	44.1	34.2	25.9	16.4	11.5	6.2	3.5	2.5
Portfolio Investment	19.3	18.1	14.1	9.8	8.9	6.4	4.6	2.8	1.9	1.3
Canada's Liabilities										
Direct Investment	108.9	90.7	78.8	68.9	61.6	48.3	43.3	26.4	17.4	12.9
Portfolio Investment	182.8	163.1	115.1	98.3	69.7	57.8	34.1	14.9	10.1	7.9
Canada's Net Foreign Liabilities										
Direct Investment	47.7	37.5	34.7	34.7	35.7	31.9	31.8	20.2	13.9	10.4
Portfolio Investment	163.5	145.0	100.4	88.5	60.8	51.4	29.5	12.1	8.2	6.6
Other Net Liabilities*	16.8	11.6	10.0	7.6	9.8	4.3	-2.4	-2.4	-0.2	-0.8
Total Net Indebtedness	228.0	194.1	145.1	130.8	106.3	87.6	58.9	29.9	21.9	16.2

Technical Notes:

1. Direct investment refers to investment made to acquire a lasting interest in an enterprise operating in a country other than that of the residence of the investor. The investor's purpose is to have an effective voice in the management of the foreign enterprise. The incorporated or unincorporated enterprise—subsidiary, affiliate or branch—in which direct investment is made is referred to as a direct investment enterprise. Direct investment is normally identified by ownership of at least 10% of the equity. Direct investment covers the long-term capital provided by or accruing to direct investors, comprising both long-term debt (bonds, debentures, loans, advances, et cetera) and equity (common and preferred shares, and retained earnings).

2. Canadian portfolio asset figures exclude net official monetary assets, non-bank holdings of short-term funds abroad, net foreign currency asset positions of chartered banks, and miscellaneous investment. On the liabilities side, the figures exclude non-resident equity in Canadian dollars, and chartered banks' net foreign currency liability position. Thus the figures in this table are long-term asset, liability, and net liability positions.

3. "Other Net Liabilities" refers to the net amount of those components of international indebtedness other than direct investment and all short-term and miscellaneous items noted above as excluded from portfolio investment. A negative "Other Net Liability" is a net asset position in this category.

Sources: Statistics Canada, *Canada's International Investment Position*, Catalogue No. 67202; Table 1.

industry than to tax factors. For example, foreign-owned subsidiaries have shut down, mature subsidiaries have seen their growth level off, and in some cases foreign interests have been bought out by domestic firms.

Figure 2.2
The Canadian International Investment position
by Relative Share of Portfolio and Direct Investment

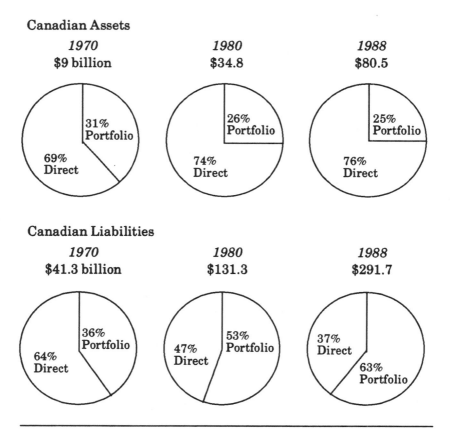

Canadian Assets

| 1970 | 1980 | 1988 |
| $9 billion | $34.8 | $80.5 |

31% Portfolio / 69% Direct

26% Portfolio / 74% Direct

25% Portfolio / 76% Direct

Canadian Liabilities

| 1970 | 1980 | 1988 |
| $41.3 billion | $131.3 | $291.7 |

36% Portfolio / 64% Direct

53% Portfolio / 47% Direct

37% Direct / 63% Portfolio

The increasing proportion of Canadian liabilities in the form of portfolio investment is representative of the general world trend in international investment. Similar analyses for all industrialized nations, including the so-called newly industrialized countries, would show comparable patterns in the direct:portfolio mix. The overall volume of international investment is increasing and, within the expanded volume, portfolio capital is growing much more rapidly than direct investment.

Summary Remarks

Taxation affects domestic and foreign investors' yields on investment. As a result, taxation affects a nation's equilibrium ratio of foreign to domestic stocks of capital. This, in turn, determines the equilibrium stock of capital and thus the ratio of capital to other productive factors such as labour.

Capital stock adjustments occur via flows. However, the simplicity of the stock/ flow distinction is potentially deceiving in analysis of the benefits and costs of policy regarding foreign investment. Flows are obviously small relative to stocks. Nevertheless, the immediate effects of tax policy on flows are proportionately larger and may be of more serious concern than the longer-run tax effect on equilibrium stocks. For example, abrupt changes in flows of foreign capital have secondary effects involving the exchange rate which may be as significant for the open economy as the contribution of the capital flow to the change in capital stock.

The immediate impact of foreign borrowing on the exchange rate depends primarily on the use to which the foreign-borrowed funds are put. For example, when the Canadian government (or a large domestic corporation) borrows abroad and converts the foreign funds to Canadian dollars to spent in Canada, say on Canadian-produced capital goods or a construction project, the creation of the foreign liability—the imported capital—puts pressure on the value of the Canadian dollar. An increase in the foreign exchange value of the Canadian dollar makes our exports less attractive on world markets whilst discouraging imports.[4] On the other hand, if a Canadian government or a Canadian firm borrows abroad to finance foreign purchases—for example, if Air Canada borrows in New York to purchase an American-built aircraft—no immediate foreign exchange transaction occurs. Canada simply incurs a long-term obligation to sell Canadian dollars (purchase United States dollars) periodically in order to service the foreign debt. Nevertheless the foreign exchange market will anticipate the future series of transactions and the negative impact on the value of the Canadian dollar. A foreign financial liability sooner or later requires an increase in Canadian exports to provide foreign exchange to service and retire the financial obligation. As a practical matter, however, even if foreign borrowing for domestic expenditures and foreign borrowing for imports ultimately imply similar increases in foreign liabilities, their respective impacts on the exchange rate may differ depending on the composition and timing of buy and sell pressures on our currency.[5]

Tax policy that affects the cost of borrowing abroad thus potentially affects the exchange rate—via the impact on the volume of net borrowing—and such effects on the exchange rate may have important repercussions in sectors beyond those employing the foreign capital directly. The crucial interaction of international trade and international investment are examined in greater detail in the following chapter.

3.

The Symmetry of Taxes on Trade and Taxes on Capital

Introduction

International efficiency derived from the unrestricted flow of capital has a counterpart in the efficiency of free trade. The purpose of this chapter is to establish the parallel between the economic benefits from international capital movements and the more traditional gains from trade and, further, to illustrate that the well-known consequences of restrictive policies on trade can be replicated through the taxation of international portfolio capital.

As already mentioned, gains from trade constitute a venerable focus for efficiency in international economics. In the pure trade model, international competition allocates production to lowest cost producers and delivers goods to those who value them most. World economic welfare is thus maximized through specialization of production, division of labour, and economies of scale.

The free trade proposition assumes an international adjustment mechanism involving flexible relative prices within nations and, usually, flexible exchange rates between nations. Flexible internal and external prices serve to clear national and international markets. (Free trade also results in global efficiency when exchange rates are fixed, but this entails a more complex adjustment mechanism involving internal inflation or deflation.) Frictionless price adjustments, could they be attained, ensure the compatibility of international economic integration with full employment in each country's resources even if those national factors are not internationally mobile.

Essentially, if factors such as capital or labour are internationally immobile, international production and patterns of trade—in the absence of barriers to trade—adjust to achieve world efficiency in view of world prices. Nations export goods and services for which they have comparative advantage and they import goods and services that are produced more efficiently elsewhere. Comparative advantage dictates that a nation will export goods that intensively require the factor of production that the nation has in relative abundance. For example, a nation with a relative abundance of capital will export capital-intensive goods and it will import labour-intensive goods.

The interesting questions in trade arise when the imperfect world is at odds with the pure trade model. Tariffs, quotas, and other interventions in trade tend to cause production costs to differ from marginal user valuations (product prices) across countries, thus creating welfare losses. Trade barriers result in reduced global output and, within countries, they give rise to loss of productive efficiency and redistributions of income.

The trade principle that dictates that exports intensively use the factor that a nation has in abundance suggests an alternative arrangement when factors are mobile. Export the factor. In terms of international production efficiency, the factor-abundance principle that determines the direction and composition of trade is analogous to the model outlined in the previous chapter that describes the direction and extent of international capital movements.

When capital is internationally mobile, a symmetry emerges between the distortions in international capital allocation caused by taxation and the more conventional distortions in trade. Establishing the parallel is convenient for policy analysis. For example, the "small country : large country" distinction so fundamental to analysis of interventions in trade, appears equally relevant with respect to distortions in international capital markets. Moreover, due to the increasing integration of international financial markets, capital can move more rapidly than goods. This creates the real likelihood that, in a reversal of the historic roles of the real and financial sides of the international economy, portfolio capital movements are the driving force for trade.

The Linkage Between International Trade and Portfolio Capital

In order to establish the fundamental symmetry between taxation of trade and taxation of portfolio capital, and especially to demonstrate that policies that inhibit international capital flows have a counterpart in traditional trade barriers, it is useful first to identify how trade and foreign capital flows are linked. In this section we outline the basic macroeconomic accounting identities that relate domestic spending and production to savings, consumption, and investment and thence to the capital and current accounts of the Balance of Payments.

Flows of international portfolio capital in or out of one nation largely represent the difference between that nation's income and its expenditure on consumption and investment. When a country spends more than its current income, as the United States has in recent years, the so-called external imbalance is reflected simultaneousiy in a current account deficit (dollars flowing out) and capital inflows (dollars flowing in). The Balance of Payments must *balance*. Capital inflows finance current account (predominantly trade) deficits. Current account surpluses, on the other hand, generate excess foreign receipts that are then used to purchase foreign assets; that is, trade surpluses give rise to capital exports. From a savings perspective, capital inflows augment domestic savings while capital exports represent an overflow of domestic savings into foreign markets.

In general, profligate nations partially finance their consumption and investment by selling financial assets abroad. On the other hand, high saving nations accumulate financial assets of trade-deficit nations; that is, nations with surplus savings export capital. Capital inflows (outflows) arise when the domestic rate of savings is too low (high) for external balance. Since domestic savings is a residual, external imbalance can likewise be viewed as the rate of consumption being too high or too low. The following paragraphs present the relations explicitly.

National income, which is the same as national product, is either spent on consumption or it is saved:

National
income   =   Consumption   +   Savings

The total amount that a nation spends on goods and services is its national expenditure. Such spending is either for consumption or domestic real investment. Real investment refers to expenditures on plant and equipment, research and development, or similar outlays designed to increase national productive capacity. In terms of expenditure:

National   Domestic
expenditure   =   Consumption   +   investment

If national expenditure is subtracted from national income, consumption nets out and a third relation is established:

National   National   Domestic
income   –   expenditure   =   Savings   –   investment

To the extent that national income exceeds expenditure, national savings exceed domestic investment. In an open economy the surplus savings must be invested abroad. (On the other hand, in a closed economy surplus savings bring about lower interest rates which in turn spur investment to the point that ultimately restores equality of savings and investment.) Thus domestic savings in an open economy are allocated to domestic investment and net foreign investment:

                Domestic   Net foreign
Savings   –   investment   =   investment

Net foreign investment, of course, may be either positive or negative depending on whether domestic savings are greater or less than domestic investment. If savings are smaller, capital inflows represent foreign savings used to finance the excess of domestic investment over domestic savings. On the other hand, domestic savings in excess of investment are used to purchase (foreign) assets of deficit-saving nations. These transactions are recorded in the **capital account** of the Balance of Payments.

The **current account** of the Balance of Payments records the exchange of domestic currency for foreign currency. Receipts of foreign currency from exports must be respent on imported goods and services or for the purchase of foreign assets. If the current account is in deficit, that is if expenditures on imported goods and services exceed receipts from exports, the additional foreign currency is derived from the sale of domestic assets to foreigners. That is

$$\text{Net foreign investment} = \text{Exports} - \text{Imports}$$

This establishes the direct link between the balance on capital account and the balance on current account. It also establishes an important linkage between foreign capital flows and domestic savings. To make this later connection explicit, note that the excess of domestic income over expenditure on domestic goods and services must equal exports. Similarly, total expenditure minus expenditure on domestic goods and services equals imports. Netting out expenditures on domestic goods and services, the result is:

$$\text{National income} - \text{National expenditure} = \text{Exports} - \text{Imports}$$

In summary:

$$\text{Savings} - \text{Domestic investment} = \text{Exports} - \text{Imports} = \text{Net foreign investment}$$

The balance on current account must equal the net capital outflow. The interpretation is straightforward. Foreign currency earned by selling goods and services abroad must be either spent on imports or exchanged for claims against foreigners. If the current account is in surplus then the nation is a net exporter of capital; on the other hand, a current account deficit is financed with capital imports.

In anticipation of the analysis of the following section, it is perhaps evident from this discussion that policy interventions, such as tariffs or quotas designed to deal with a trade imbalance will correspondingly be reflected in the capital account. Likewise policy interventions directed to international capital flows, such as taxes on interest paid to foreigners, will correspondingly be reflected in the trade balance.

External Imbalances: What Leads?
What Follows?

The identities of the Balance of Payments do not reveal the under-lying economic forces that are give rise to external imbalances and then lead to subsequent adjustments to restore equilibrium. For example, although a trade deficit involves a corresponding inflow of capital, that identity does not shed light on the question of which comes first—the trade imbalance or the inflow of foreign capital. In traditional approaches to trade, it is generally assumed that the forces of trade are predominant, based as they are in real con-siderations such as comparative advantage, technology, tastes, and the distribution of natural and national endowments. If trade is predominant, then capital flows accommodate trade imbalances.

Recent international experience, however, points to an emerging predominance of role of portfolio capital. It appears that trade now adjusts to international capital imbalances rather than vice versa. For example, as a result of the expansionary fiscal and deflationary monetary policy mix in the United States, the U.S. domestic savings rate dropped sharply through the 1980s; real interest rates remained high as an enormous influx of foreign funds buoyed the level of the U.S. dollar. The result is a squeeze on the U.S. traded goods sector: export and import-competing industries in the U.S. have had to contract relative to nontraded sectors. This, of course, fuels the fires of protectionism. In essence, the U.S. dollar is "overvalued" in the sense that the capital account has been driving the current account; the dollar has risen because of capital influx which, in turn, has affected the volume and composition of trade.

Similarly in Canada, the tight anti-inflationary monetary stance of the Bank of Canada, the "Status-Crow" through late 1988 until early 1990, drove real Canadian interest rates to an unpre-cedented level above U.S. real rates. The strong demand for Canadian dollars to purchase Canadian financial assets—inflows of portfolio capital—pushed up the international value of the Canadian dollar with inevitable effects on trade. The traditional Canadian visible trade surplus fell sharply and, at one point, visible trade was in deficit.

Problems of the type just outlined are becoming systemic. The integration of financial markets in industrialized world creates the potential for significant capital-account-driven changes in exchange rates with subsequent impacts on the volume and composition of trade. Indeed, the world is awash with stateless capital. The sheer volume of funds in international portfolio capital markets, funds that are rapidly directed to sources of higher interest, accentuate the vulnerability of the international trading system to the volatility of exchange rates.

Thus the following examination of taxes on foreign capital, which is posed in an analytic framework analogous to the model used to explain trade tariffs, is particularly relevant in a world in which traditional tariffs structures are being dismantled and, in their place, protectionist policies are implemented through taxes on factors of production, especially capital.

A Simple Model of Taxes on Imported Capital

The discussion above outlined how a country that spends more than it earns, or invests more than it saves, must derive the additional required finance from foreign sources. This essentially describes a state of disequilibrium—a country cannot continuously run a current account deficit (or surplus) matched by an equally continuous inflow (or outflow) of capital. Other factors, such as changes in domestic interest rates and/or the exchange rate eventually come into play to restore equilibrium in the markets that govern international trade and international finance.

In the following analysis, we change the approach from partial to general equilibrium in order to address the more or less permanent effects that arise from taxation of internationally mobile capital. The purpose is to demonstrate a fundamental symmetry between tariffs on imported goods and taxes on imported capital.

To begin, assume a small country that produces only one good with capital and labour. Capital is assumed to be mobile between countries but labour is immobile. The major economic implication of this depiction of the world is that one interest rate prevails internationally, and hence the equilibrium return on capital is exogenous or given from the perspective of the individual country.

The domestic demand curve for capital is the marginal value product of capital shown as DD' in Figure 3.1. As in the model developed in the previous chapter, the domestic demand curve for capital is downward sloping to reflect its diminishing marginal product. The domestic supply curve, SS', relates the rate of return to the quantity of domestic capital supplied. With the prevailing world rate of return to capital fixed at OR, the domestic demand for capital is RD and domestic supply is RS. The difference, SD, is imported from abroad. RS is therefore domestically-owned, domestically-employed capital, while SD is domestically-employed capital owned by foreigners.

Figure 3.1
A Tax on Imported Capital

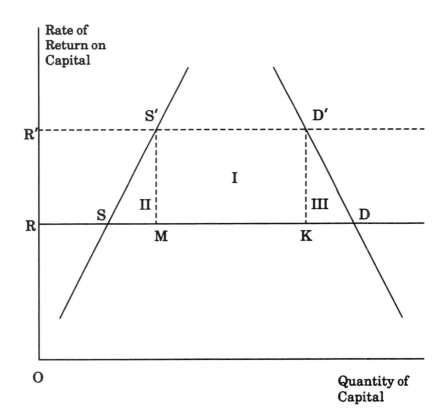

Consider a tax on capital imports. From the point of view of non-resident investors, this tax—like the interest withholding tax in Canada (Brean, 1984b)—initially reduces the after-tax rate of return from capital invested in the capital-importing nation relative to the rate of return available elsewhere. Accordingly, foreign capital will be withdrawn from the domestic market, thus driving up the gross return until the net-of-tax return equals the world rate of return. Since the latter is by definition fixed, the gross return to capital in the capital-importing nation must rise to the full extent of the tax.

In Figure 3.1, we assume a tax on capital imports imposed at the rate RR'/OR. Foreign-owned capital will then leave the country until the gross domestic return on capital rises to OR'. This equals the world rate of return net of tax. Capital imports from abroad therefore fall from DS to D'S'. As the gross return to capital rises domestically, additional domestically-owned capital (which, of course, is *not* subject to the tax) will be supplied. The end result, however, is less capital used by domestic industry. The supply of domestically-owned capital increases from RS to R'S', while the total amount of capital used domestically falls from DR to D'R'.

The increase in the gross return to capital means that domestic owners of capital—who do *not* pay the tax—gain from the tax at the same time that domestic users of capital lose. The gain is RR'S'S while the loss is RR'D'D. Of the difference between these two areas—the trapezoid S'D'DS—the amount represented by area I goes to the government in the form of tax revenues. The net difference—the sum of areas II and III—therefore represents the pure economic loss or welfare cost of the tax on capital imports.

A conventional analysis of a general tariff on imported goods would yield similar results including a revenue flow to government, real gains for sectors producing import substitutes, and real losses to those who use imported goods for intermediate or final consumption. Our analysis thus shows that the effects of a tax on capital imports and a tariff are symmetrical, provided there is at least some degree of elasticity of domestic capital supply with respect to the rate of return on capital.

There is one important difference between a tax on capital imports and a tariff. In the case of a tariff, the increase in the price of the imported commodity is unambiguously borne by the domestic consumer; the consumer cannot shift the burden of the tax. In the case of a tax on capital imports, however, the increase in the price of capital, in the circumstances assumed here, will be shifted by the domestic user of capital onto *labour*, the specific (or immobile) factor of production. Thus, rather than damage foreign investors, a tax on capital imports potentially effects a purely internal transfer of income, from domestic labour to domestic capital and, perhaps, to the government if there is a net gain in tax revenue. What appears to be a tax on foreigners turns out in fact to be a tax on domestic labour.

The Foreign Tax Credit

The analysis of a tax on capital imports changes substantially if the residence country (the home of the foreign investors) gives full and immediate credit for taxes that foreign investors pay in the source country (the capital-importing country). In that case a tax on capital imports will have no effect on either domestic users or domestic suppliers of capital, since there will then be no tax reason for foreign investors to withdraw capital. What foreign investors pay to the government of the source country in tax is received back from the residence government in the form of credit against residence taxes. Indeed, the only effect of a tax on capital imports in this case is to transfer income from the residence government to the government of the source country.[6] Thus, for example, if Canada places a tax on capital imports and the United States gives a full tax credit to American investors in Canada for taxes that they must pay to the Canadian government, the effect of the tax is to transfer income from the United States Treasury to the Receiver General of Canada. A reduction in the Canadian tax in these circumstances will obviously reverse the direction of this transfer. If the U.S. foreign tax credit does not fully neutralize such taxes, however, the effects are closer to those described in the previous paragraph.

It is in fact unlikely that a Canadian withholding tax on interest paid on Canadian bonds held by foreign investors would be fully offset by a foreign tax credit in the residence country.[7] The foreign tax credit allowed American foreign investors, for example, would be insufficient in most cases due to the structure of the credit. A withholding tax is generally assessed on *gross* interest payments that leave the source country whereas the foreign tax credit calculation is based on *net* foreign source income. Net foreign source income refers to the spread between interest earned on loans (in Canada) and interest paid on the American financial institution's liabilities to support the loan. The base for determining foreign tax credits is therefore only a fraction of the base for determining the withholding tax. As a result, insofar as withholding taxes exceed offsetting credits, portfolio capital flows are choked off and Canadian interest rates rise as explained in the model. In other circumstances, foreign tax credits are irrelevant to holders of foreign bonds. Large volumes of international portfolio capital represent the investments of such tax exempt funds as pensions, trusts, and foundations for which tax credits are useless inasmuch as they face no residence tax liability in the first place. Finally, the recent significant reductions in the United States corporate tax rate along with the general tightening of American rules governing the foreign tax credit increase the likelihood that the credit will not fully eliminate the bite of a Canadian tax on interest income.

Relative Size Is Crucial

Despite the obvious oversimplification of the symmetry between trade protection and capital-import protection, this brief discussion contains a potentially important message for policy makers in open economies. It is difficult to tax internationally mobile factors of production effectively either with an internal tax (such as the corporate income tax) or an external tax (such as the interest withholding tax). No matter which factor bears the legal burden of a tax, in small open economies the least mobile factor—usually labour—will wind up bearing the burden in fact. The stickiness of real world adjustment mechanisms may mute this outcome, particularly in the case of direct investment, but its long-run validity can hardly be in doubt where portfolio investment is concerned.

The Belgian Circle

The smallest countries are especially vulnerable. Belgium, for example, imposes a non-creditable withholding tax on interest earned by Belgians on most savings accounts and financial assets. As a result, a substantial amount of Belgian savings flows abroad —for example, to Luxembourg and the Netherlands—to avoid the withholding tax. Some of these funds are eventually used by the Luxembourgois and Dutch financial institutions (including foreign branches of Belgian banks) to purchase securities issued by the Belgian government or Belgian corporations. Foreigners are exempt from the tax. The net effect, ironic as well as inefficient, is that the withholding tax forces Belgian financial intermediation to operate through foreign centers.

The outflow of Belgian savings together with the general inefficiency of the arrangement puts upward pressure on Belgian interest rates and thus shifts the burden of the tax on to immobile factors such as labour. Belgian domestic interest rates, however, are not higher by the full amount of the tax; some Belgian savers who cannot avoid taxable accounts bear the tax. The Belgian authorities have found it politically difficult to unravel this set-up primarily because of the resistance of Belgian banks which by now have a strong vested interest in the complex arrangements induced by the tax. Pressure for tax harmonization from the European Community, together with objective external advice from the International Monetary Fund, led to a recent reduction in the tax rate from 25 percent to 10 percent.

Germany: On Again, Off Again

Taxes on internationally mobile capital can be expected to induce changes in the structure of finance. Such changes generally shift borrowing away from taxed securities to untaxed securities. In this respect, recent German experience provides another example of the high degree of responsiveness of international investment to tax changes. In the Fall of 1987 the West German government announced that a withholding tax on interest income would go into effect in January 1989. The tax was initially proposed to be a 15 percent levy applied to both resident and non-resident investors in German bond markets. While German domestic bonds (including government bonds) were subject to the tax, foreign securities issued in Germany were exempt. Soon after the announcement, both resident (West German) and non-resident investors reduced their purchases of German assets. In contrast, Deutsche Mark bonds issued by foreign borrowers were much in demand. These shifts in demand promptly gave rise to corresponding changes in interest rate differentials between taxable German bonds and other similar but untaxed securities. For example, the yield on German Federal bonds historically was 250 to 500 basis points below the yield on Deutsche Bonds in the Euromarkets; following the announcement of the withholding tax, the yields on German Federal bonds rose above the yield on foreign DM bonds in the Euromarkets.

In April 1989 the German government announced that the withholding tax would be repealed by mid-year. The authorities cited serious adverse effects on monetary policy and the German capital markets due to the tax. Following the announcement, the previous tax-induced adjustments in the capital markets began to be substantially reversed. Both domestic and foreign investors shifted their portfolios toward German bond issues. By May 1989 the yield on German Federal bonds fell back below that on Euromarket Deutsche Mark bonds for the first time since December 1987.

The United States and the Strategic Advantage of Size

In contrast to the examples of Canada, Belgium, and Germany, the position in a large country, such as the United States, may be quite different in terms of the scope for strategic policy vis-à-vis international capital markets. The term "large" has a specific meaning in the context of markets; a country is large if it has sufficient economic power to influence prices in the international markets that it enters either as a large supplier or a large demander. For example, Canada is considered to be large in world uranium markets, South Africa is large in gold, Saudi Arabia is large in oil, and as a demander of traded goods the United States is large in virtually all commodities.

The United States is perhaps the only country with the potential to effectively impose tax on international capital to its own national advantage. The U.S. is hardly a small actor in world financial markets. In a recent count, securities issued by the United States amounted to more than 14 percent of the total value of securities issued by the OECD nations. As Goulder (1989) suggests, this large share of the supply side of the market indicates considerable monopsony power: changes in the U.S. demand for investible funds have a potentially significant effect on the world interest rates.

When a nation has monopsony power in international capital markets it has the potential to lower the net rate of interest paid to foreign investors. Exploiting monopsonistic power in international financial markets essentially means that the large country recognizes that foreign holders of its assets are unable to fully adjust to a reduction in after-tax return on these assets. The burden of tax on interest paid to foreign investors is at least partially borne by such holders of domestic assets, and thus the tax is not fully borne by domestic capital. As a result, a withholding tax on interest paid to foreigners will not necessarily reduce aggregate welfare in the nation that levies the withholding tax. The benefits of lower net interest rates paid on foreign capital plus the increase in tax revenue serve to offset the adverse effects of higher domestic interest rates. Of course, the welfare-improving effects of a withholding tax imposed by a large country occur only if that country in fact imports capital. It is perhaps interesting to observe a recently revived interest in withholding taxation by the United States that is coincident with the U.S. shift from being a capital-exporter to a capital-importer.

Market share is not the only potential source of market power for a large country such as the United States. If foreign investors cannot perfectly substitute U.S. securities for foreign securities, then U.S. interest rates would not necessarily rise to the point where the net of withholding tax rate of interest paid by the U.S. to foreigners equals the foreign rate of interest. In other words, the lack of alternative-to-U.S. investments would force foreign holders of U.S. securities to bear the U.S. tax through lower net of tax returns. In the extreme case, where foreigners cannot substitute foreign assets for U.S. assets to any significant degree, foreigners are strictly price-takers of U.S. net interest rates. A U.S. withholding tax on interest paid to foreigners need not cause U.S. interest rates to rise at all. On the contrary, the after-tax rate of interest received by foreign holders of U.S. assets would fall by the full amount of the tax with no reduction in the supply of foreign funds to the U.S. In that case the U.S. Treasury collects the withholding tax revenue and thus U.S. aggregate savings increase with subsequent implications for the fiscal deficit as well as the trade and capital accounts as outlined earlier.

In fact, as noted above, recent policy discussion has turned to the merits of reintroducing the U.S. withholding tax on interest paid to foreigners. Such a tax was removed in 1984 primarily because it was viewed as being an ineffective revenue source. The tax induced substantial substitution of offshore for domestic financial transactions, for example through the Netherlands Antilles, to avoid the tax otherwise levied on U.S. interest paid into the Euromarkets. When the tax was removed, security issues with the U.S. rose on a net basis from $19 billion to $50 billion within two years. The rise was due almost entirely to an increase in foreign purchases of U.S. securities, largely corporate and government bonds (Papke 1989).

The Netherlands Antilles "window" has been closed following a renegotiation of the relevant tax treaty. If the U.S. could effectively prevent similar channels from being established, it could possibly exploit its commanding position in international capital markets through an "optimal tax" on capital imports. An "optimal tax" is like having it both ways: raising tax revenue and exporting the burden.

In the trade literature, the familiar "optimal tariff" argument states that if, from a free trade position, a large country introduces an import tariff and gradually increases its rate, the tariff-imposing country's economic welfare will first increase, then reach a maximum, and then decrease as the tariff rate increases. The initial increase in national welfare stems from a terms of trade effect whereby the tariff forces foreign suppliers to reduce the world price of the goods subject to tariff in order to access the large country. However, since the volume of trade must fall, the eventual decline of the large country's welfare sets in when the tariff level causes a marginal loss of trade in excess of the self-serving effect of the lower price of imports. The tariff that maximizes economic welfare is known that the "optimum tariff".

The following sections outlines an identical argument made with respect to an optimal tax on imported capital.

Optimal Taxes on International Portfolio Capital

The rationale for an optimal tax on capital imports to a large country is illustrated in Figure 3.2. The horizontal axis represents the total amount of capital required by the domestic economy of the large country. For simplicity, the analysis focuses on the mix of domestic and foreign capital within a fixed total amount of capital employed in the large country; thus while the return on capital in that country is fixed, the analysis disaggregates the two sources of supply of capital—domestic and foreign—and postulates different cost of capital functions for these respective supplies. Also, costs are different as perceived by the capital exporting country as opposed to the vantage point of the rest of the world.

The marginal cost of domestically-owned capital in the large country is O_DMC_D, a line with an upward slope representing the fact that higher domestic yields are required to mobilize increases in domestic savings. On the other hand, the marginal cost of foreign owned capital *if used abroad* (that is, in the large country) is O_FAC_F; reading right to left from the origin O_F, this line rises for foreign capital invested in the large country because more capital in the large country leaves less capital in the rest of the world. Although O_FAC_F is a marginal cost for the rest of the world, it represents the *average* cost of foreign owned capital in the large country because it pays a single rate on all the capital it imports. Finally, as always the case with rising average cost, the marginal cost of capital is above average cost as perceived by the large country; O_FMC_F is above O_FAC_F. The more capital the large country imports, the higher the price it must pay for it.

In order to maximize its economic welfare, a capital-importing country should equate the marginal cost of domestically-owned capital and the marginal cost of foreign-owned capital *to it*. This occurs at point A in Figure 3.2, with O_DN domestic capital and NO_F foreign capital used to satisfy domestic capital requirements. But while A maximizes domestic economic welfare, world welfare would be maximized at point B which equates the marginal cost of domestically-owned capital used at home and the marginal cost of foreign-owned capital if used abroad.

Point B would be the result in a situation of unrestricted capital imports but it is quite clear that at point B the marginal cost to the domestic country of using foreign-owned capital is greater than the marginal cost of domestically-owned capital; that is, there is too much capital import at point B. By imposing a tax on capital imports—and thus cutting back on them—the home country can gain the area ABC in comparison with the situation of free capital imports. These home country gains are, of course, the expense of more cosmopolitan welfare criteria, because, while the optimum tax on capital imports improves home welfare ABC, it reduces world welfare by ABD.

Figure 3.2
An Optimal Tax on Capital Imports

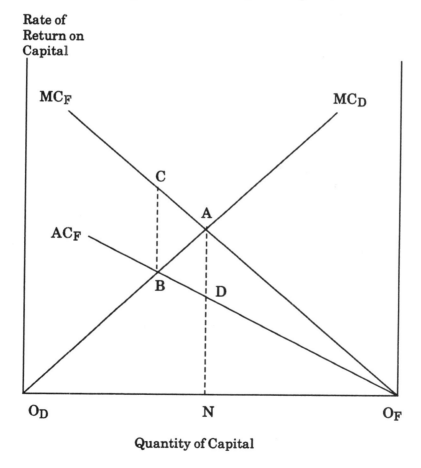

Quantity of Capital

As shown earlier, a tax on capital imports imposes an excess burden on the tax-imposing economy measured at a constant world price of capital. For a large country, however, insofar as such a tax actually *reduces* the price of capital on world markets, it includes a transfer of income from foreigners to the domestic country. This international income transfer (terms-of-trade effect) is positive for the domestic country although the resulting excess burden effect on itself is, as always, negative. Starting from a point of free capital imports, if a small tax on capital imports is imposed and its rate is gradually increased, economic welfare in the tax-imposing country will first increase (the positive international income transfer effect dominates the negative excess burden effect), then reach a maximum, and finally decrease (the excess burden effect dominates the international income transfer effect) as the tax on capital imports increases. This is of course the "optimal tariff" result.

And Small Countries Too . . .

Somewhat paradoxically, there may also be a plausible case for a small country to impose a tax on its capital imports in certain instances. The problem is posed in an intertemporal context. Additional foreign borrowing increases the stream of debt service payments that eventually flows abroad. Such payments are settled in foreign exchange that must be derived from exports. Thus, increased use of foreign capital creates a need for increased future exports and, therefore, an eventual deterioration of the terms of trade facing a small country. Burgess' (1985) simulation of this phenomenon indicates that the adverse terms of trade effect may be quite high for Canada, a consideration that suggests it is potentially in Canada's best interest to tax non-residents' capital income but not residents'. Of course, this trade deterioration increases the burden of public sector debt accumulation which leads to accumulation of foreign liabilities. Such a policy, of course, would also assume, questionably, that the neighbours being so beggared would not retaliate!

The Optimal Tax on Capital Exports

A large country may find itself in a situation where a tax on capital *exports*, like an "optimal" tax on capital imports, improves its welfare at some economic cost to other countries. A country with the potential to export sufficient capital to the rest of the world as to affect world interest rates faces a less than perfectly elastic demand for its capital. In other words, the more capital that is exported from the large country, the lower is the average rate of return on such capital placed abroad. Thus, the marginal unit of exported capital lowers the rate of return on all previous foreign investment.

The marginal investor does not take account of the losses on the inframarginal investments although clearly the losses are relevant to the social rate of return of the capital exporting nation. Indeed, the social rate of return is equal to the gain on the marginal unit less the losses on the inframarginal units. Therefore, because of the downward slope of the demand curve, the marginal rate of return on exported capital must always be less than the average rate of return.

The capital exporting nation may maximize its own welfare by permitting exports only up to the point where the marginal rate of return on its foreign investment is equal to this opportunity cost of capital in domestic use. This optimal tax strategy involves a capital export tax equal to the difference between the domestic and foreign rates of return in equilibrium—an "interest equalization tax". Thus, restricting capital exports would leave the private marginal return on foreign investment above the return on domestic investment and would also leave the large country with lower than world average rates of return as well. Although the capital exporting nation can thus improve its welfare, the world as a whole is less well off because the export tax restricts international capital allocation and prevents the equalization of the marginal productivity of capital in all countries.

Terms of Trade Effects

A country that imports capital must eventually repay the foreign debt. A country that exports capital is eventually repaid. As we have noted earlier, the retirement of foreign debt has implications for the exchange rate through the time pattern of buy and sell pressures on the domestic currency. For example, a debtor country's terms of trade—the price of its exports relative to its imports—could deteriorate due to the future flow of payments to retire foreign borrowing. This negative effect offsets an initial positive impact due to the original inflow of capital. There is some question of whether the relatively short and sharp initial positive impact of foreign investment on the exchange rate weighs more or less heavily than the smaller but more protracted negative effects that follow. Explicit account of the effects of international capital movements on the exchange rate and on the terms of trade raises additional considerations for the use of tax to encourage positive national benefits or to discourage negative effects.

Keynes long ago recognized the underpinnings of optimal taxes on internationally mobile capital, in particular the impact of capital flows on the terms of trade. Keynes noted that:

> Foreign investment does not automatically expand our exports by a corresponding amount. It so affects the foreign exchanges that we are compelled to export more in order to maintain our solvency. It may be the case—I fancy that it is now the case—that we can only do this by lowering the price of our products in terms of the products of other nations, that is by allowing the ratio of real interchange to move to our disadvantage. (Keynes, 1924)

An empirical analysis by Whalley (1982), done at a time when the United States was in fact a capital exporter, suggests that the United States gains from taxing capital because its corporate tax produces significant positive terms of trade effects. More recently, and noting that the United States is now a net capital importing nation, Goulder (1990) argues that a reintroduction of the U.S. withholding tax on interest paid to foreigners, if not accompanied by similar (retaliatory) tax measures by foreign governments, would yield aggregate domestic economic benefits for the United States. The U.S. gains are in the first instance attributable to U.S. financial market power and to induced increases in U.S. domestic savings. By raising U.S. pre-tax rates of return on investment relative to foreign rates, a U.S. withholding tax would reduce U.S. domestic investment relative to foreign investment. Over time, this suppression of investment reduces the relative supply of U.S. goods and raises their relative price in world markets—an effect that boosts the real exchange rate. A higher exchange rate is necessary for trade balance. The higher external value of the U.S. dollar means that the U.S. would have to export less in order to meet its obligations to foreigners.

For Canada, which is clearly a price-taker in international capital markets, analysis of optimal taxes on mobile capital as if this country initiated such policy is likely to be less relevant than consideration of taxes imposed by larger nations on their capital imports or exports.

Paradoxically, a large economy can potentially benefit from taxation of internationally mobile capital on both the demand side (as capital importer) and on the supply side (as capital exporter). To the extent that capital taxation by a large country allows it to capture benefits at the expense of its neighbours, the effects work through improved terms of trade as we have seen. Generally, as in most examples of zero-sum interventionist policy, what is best for the large country is not the best for the world taken as a whole, which gives rise to an inevitable conflict between world and national efficiency. From Canada's point of view—and from the viewpoint of the world as a whole as well—large nations should presumably be discouraged from following tax policies that discriminate against and thus restrict mobile capital. Little countries however have little clout. Under the "rules of the game" discussed below, their best bet is to negotiate international tax agreements on a bilateral basis in order to increase certainty in international tax relations, to reduce the chance of pre-emptive changes by the larger nations, and to limit destructive tax escalation.

In short, the outcome of this simple analysis is that Canada, which is both an importer and an exporter of capital, seems best advised to follow as neutral a policy towards taxation of international flows as possible: on the capital import side because it is likely to only hurt itself, and on the export side because it wants to avoid retaliation from those who can hurt it. The main qualification to this conclusion is the credit mechanism in foreign countries, the importance of which is discussed further below. First, however, Chapter 4 sets out the current rules under which the international tax game is played—rules that are closely related to the arguments set out above.

4.

Attaining Neutrality: National Tax Policy

As explained in Chapter 2, the interaction of domestic and foreign tax systems determines effective tax differentials between returns to domestic and foreign investment. International differentials in after-tax returns are driving forces in the mechanism to allocate mobile capital among countries. Other things being equal, relatively more capital settles in relatively low tax countries. This international allocative consequence of taxation is closely linked to the economic concept of efficiency. Efficient international allocation is marked by the equality of pre-tax marginal returns on capital across countries while, on the other hand, tax-induced inefficiency is synonymous with distortion or a tax wedge between alternative pre-tax returns. In general, if a tax does not distort private investment decisions it is said to be "neutral".

Despite the apparent simplicity of the criterion for neutrality, the question takes on considerable complexity in the international realm. For one thing, neutrality cannot be defined unless, from the national perspective, one defines the alternative investments at issue. One must distinguish between: (1) the alternative (domestic versus foreign) investment opportunities of domestic investors, and (2) the alternative (domestic versus foreign) investment opportunities of investors abroad. International tax arrangements can either establish a situation wherein domestic investors experience no tax distortion with respect to their decisions to invest at home or abroad *or* a situation wherein investors abroad will not be discriminated against (vis-à-vis domestic investors) with respect to their investments. The former arrangement is said to promote capital-export neutrality while the latter promotes capital-import neutrality.

Capital-export neutrality thus refers to the choice domestic investors face between investing at home or abroad. The interaction of domestic and foreign taxes is capital-export neutral if domestic investors are indifferent between domestic and foreign investments with equal pre-tax yields. As already demonstrated, capital-export neutrality is established when *inter alia* the capital-exporting country taxes its investors' worldwide income on a current basis at the "residence" rate (the rate in the capital-exporters' country) with full and immediate credit for taxes paid abroad. If a country maintains capital-export neutrality, its capital is allocated efficiently throughout the world—a contribution to world economic efficiency. However, as the discussion of optimal tax strategies made clear, *global* allocative efficiency is not necessarily consistent with maximum *national* benefit from foreign investment. While capital-export neutrality is an international efficiency criterion, it is by no means necessarily an appropriate policy goal.

Capital-import neutrality, on the other hand, takes the perspective of the capital-importing nation. Taxation is capital-import neutral, for example, if Canadian investors and foreign investors receive equal after-tax yields from an identical investment in Canada. In other words, capital-import neutrality places domestic investors and foreign investors on an equal tax footing with respect to investment in the capital-importing country. It is achieved when the capital-importing nation taxes income from foreign-owned investment at the same rate as domestically-owned investment and the capital-exporting nation exempts foreign-source income from (residence) taxation.

For both capital-export and capital-import neutrality, the focus of policy is on the *overall* tax rate on investment, inclusive of levies of both source and residence jurisdictions. The policies differ in regard to which tax rate, domestic or foreign, predominates.

(They also differ in that only capital export neutrality results in international allocative efficiency unless the tax rates are the same.) For capital-export neutrality the domestic tax rate predominates, while for capital-import neutrality it is the foreign rate(s). International tax distortion of investment decisions can be eliminated unilaterally by the potential capital-exporting country through either a foreign tax credit against the tax liability in the capital-exporting country or outright exemption of foreign-source income from tax. In the former case, capital-export neutrality is achieved; in the latter, capital-import neutrality. In either case, the capital-exporting country pays the fiscal price—it gives up tax revenue—to promote a particular international concept of economic efficiency.

In contrast, a capital-exporting country may in principle take a narrower, nationalist view of "neutrality". Counting tax revenue as part of the social return from domestic investment and noting that investors make their decisions in the light of net-of-tax returns, the national welfare of a capital-exporting nation is maximized when offshore returns *net* of foreign tax are equal to pre-tax domestic returns. The implication is that nations intent on maximizing national welfare—and not international welfare— should treat foreign taxes just like any other cost of doing business abroad. Foreign taxes are then deducted, not credited, against the residence liability (Musgrave, 1969).

The foreign tax credit attains capital-export neutrality only if offshore income is subject to residence tax rules as the foreign source income is earned. To the extent that residence assessment of tax on offshore income is in fact deferred, either by explicit provision of residence tax law or through other opportunities to delay assessment, such deferred tax payments are effectively smaller tax payments in terms of their present value. Deferral of the residence liability is a feature, for example, of the United States' tax treatment of active business income of foreign subsidiaries of American corporations. There is substantial evidence to indicate that the deferral provision discourages the repatriation of subsidiary earnings while encouraging the reinvestment of such earnings outside the United States in jurisdictions with lower tax rates (Hartman, 1985). If repatriation is deferred indefinitely, the credit system becomes equivalent to an exemption system and subsequent reinvestment earnings are subject only to foreign taxes. The ultimate allocative consequence of deferral is thus capital-import neutrality for direct investment rather than the capital-export neutrality which presumably the arrangement was originally intended to attain. On the other hand, the absence of deferral on foreign portfolio investment income is an important reason for treating it separately from direct investment as we do here.

Social Returns and Private Returns

Private investors, as individuals, are not concerned with neutrality or allocative efficiency. Investors' decisions in the face of alternative investments will equate after-tax returns in pursuit of private gain, without regard for allocative consequences. Tax rates and rules are parameters in their private investment decisions since private returns are simply after-tax returns.

Although categorically distinct from such private returns, taxes on capital income nevertheless are part of the return on capital. An all-inclusive measure defined as the social return on capital equals the private after-tax return plus taxes, or simply the pre-tax return. The social return on domestically employed capital is divided between the private investor and the government.[8] In the case of foreign investment, however, since taxes may be collected by two countries, the division of tax revenue between two countries has a significant bearing on the international division of social returns from portfolio capital.

The international division of tax revenue derived from investment is determined by the relative tax rates in the source and residence countries together with the residence country's method of foreign tax relief. The alternative methods of foreign tax relief are no relief, foreign tax deduction, foreign tax credit, and exemption. Table 4.1 shows private returns, tax flows to the residence country, and the social return to the residence country under the alternative methods.

Table 4.1 and the following discussion are based on the realistic assumption that the source country takes an initial bite of tax on income from foreign investment within its jurisdiction both through taxes on corporate income and, especially important in the case of portfolio investment, by means of source withholding taxes.

Considering first the social return to the residence country, it is clear that the notional calculation is the same regardless of the method of foreign tax relief. The social benefit of investment abroad (the residence nation's perspective) is the income available to be split between the private foreign investor and the residence nation's Treasury. The residence social rate of return is thus simply the net-of-source-tax return.

Table 4.1
Alternative Methods of Foreign Tax Relief
in Residence Countries

A.   Private Foreign Investor's Returns:

No Foreign Tax Relief: $r_s (1 - t_s - t_r)$

Foreign Tax Deduction: $r_s (1 - t_s) (1 - t_r)$

Foreign Tax Credit: $r_s (1 - t_r)$ <u>or</u> $r_s (1 - t_s)$ as $t_r \gtrless t_s$

Exemption: $r_s (1 - t_s)$

B.   Tax Revenue to Residence Country:

No Foreign Tax Relief: $t_r r_s$

Foreign Tax Deduction: $t_r r_s (1 - t_s)$

Foreign Tax Credit: $t_r r_s - t_s r_s = r_s (t_r - t_s)$

Exemption: 0

A + B. Social Return to Residence Country:

No Foreign Tax Relief: $r_s (1 - t_s)$

Foreign Tax Deduction: $r_s (1 - t_s)$

Foreign Tax Credit: $r_s (1 - t_s)$

Exemption: $r_s (1 - t_s)$

r_s = rate of return in (foreign) source country

t_r = rate of tax on capital income in the residence country

t_s = rate of tax on capital income in the source country

The social rate of return from inward foreign portfolio investment (the source nation's perspective) in this accounting is simply the source tax rate (t_s).

Since the social rate of return in the residence country does not depend on the method of foreign tax relief, the components of the social return—the private return and the tax flow to the residence country—may appear to be perfect substitutes. However, as far as economic incentives to invest abroad are concerned, the net-of-*all*-tax private return on foreign investment for a given value of r_s is obviously lowest when there is no foreign tax relief, higher with the foreign tax deduction, and highest with the (fully utilizable) foreign tax credit or exemption. This is obviously because the residence treasury is absorbing no, some, and all foreign taxes paid in the respective cases. The policies of no foreign tax relief and foreign tax deduction result in an effective source-plus-residence tax rate which is greater than the rate of tax on domestic investment in the residence country. Foreign investment is correspondingly less than, say, with the foreign tax credit. Of course, as noted earlier, this result does *not* mean that such a credit is better than a policy of deduction from the residence national point of view; to reach this conclusion one would have to show that $r_s (1 - t_s)$ is greater than the pre-tax residence return.

Policy in Practice

The general rule in the industrialized world is that in principle foreign investment income ought to be taxed at a rate which equals the domestic rate on investment that takes place at home, that is, capital-export neutrality ought to prevail. To achieve this objective, capital-exporting countries have generally been willing to provide credits for taxes paid in source countries. While this is consistent with efficient international allocation of capital, the widespread use of the policy of crediting foreign taxes is more a reflection of priorities of access to income rather than pursuit of the loftier objective of allocative efficiency. To put it simply, capital-importing countries are in the privileged position of having first kick at the can. If capital-importing countries were to refrain from taxing foreign-owned investments, this would likewise be consistent with capital export neutrality but at an obviously fiscal cost to the source countries. The dominant foreign tax credit arrangement thus results from a dual commitment to the *residence principle* of international taxation and the principle of capital-export neutrality.

The distinction between foreign direct and portfolio investment again introduces an important qualification here. While the working rules of international taxation in the developed world enable source countries to have first go at direct investment, residence countries make a strong claim of the right to effectively tax foreign portfolio investment in that a major aim of tax treaties is significantly to restrict withholding taxes.

In theory, capital-export neutrality results from a universally applied foreign-source tax credit if all foreign-source taxes are creditable, if foreign-source income is taxed (and credits allowed) on a *current* basis by the residence jurisdiction, and if the structure of taxes applied to corporate income is essentially the same everywhere. In practice, each of these three necessary conditions, to a greater or lesser degree, is lacking. Capital export neutrality is compromised by *limitations* of the tax credit, by the effects of differential personal-corporate tax *integration*, and, in the case of direct investments, by *deferral* of taxes on foreign source income.

If, for example, a capital-exporting jurisdiction does not specify an upper limit on the credit it allows for taxes paid to other jurisdictions by its residents, the doors of its treasury are wide open. An upper limit is invariably imposed on the foreign tax credit to restrict potential revenue loss, usually by stipulating that the credit cannot exceed the amount of residence tax liability otherwise due on foreign-source income. Foreign investments are thus taxed at the higher of the rates charged by the source and residence jurisdictions. If the source rate exceeds the residence rate, a tax bias prevails against capital exports (although this is strictly the case only if the residence jurisdiction adopts the *per country limitation method*, as does Canada, at least nominally).[9] Countries also usually limit tax credits to taxes similar to their own income taxes, they apply their own "sourcing" rules to allocate taxable income between jurisdictions and, in the case of portfolio investment, allow credits only for taxes directly imposed on the relevant flow of income. The latter is generally defined as *net* investment income—the yield on the (foreign) investment less the cost of funds borrowed to finance the investment.

In the case of direct investment, where many countries also extend credits for underlying corporate income taxes, *deferral* generally establishes a bias in favour of foreign direct investment if the foreign source tax rate (corporate plus withholding) is lower than the residence rate. If repatriation of foreign-source earnings is deferred indefinitely, the present value of the residence liability approaches zero. If repatriation occurs immediately, or if there is no deferral provision, the net residence liability is likewise low (zero) when the source tax rate is close to (higher than) the residence rate.

Corporate-Personal Tax Integration and International Neutrality

Finally, if capital-export neutrality is the appropriate goal of policy, how can it be achieved when different jurisdictions have substantially different systems of taxing corporations and share-holders as do the United States and Canada? Since the analysis of this question becomes complicated quickly, only a brief illustration will be given here, concentrating on the case of portfolio investment. The complexity arises from the numerous possible methods of integrating personal and corporate taxes.

Basically, to achieve neutrality in this sense of considering the tax liability through to shareholders, all foreign corporate and withholding taxes must be "grossed up" (that is, included in taxable income) and then credited to *corporate* portfolio investors, with any excess credit being refunded. Alternatively, there could be a "pass-through" to shareholders of the credit for any foreign withholding tax. However, if the corporation is considered to be the sole decision-making unit, a full credit for *both* taxes at the corporate level would be more consistent with international tax neutrality.

For *individual* portfolio investment on the other hand, what may be called a "corporate tax adjustment" is really needed in order to eliminate any tax differential that would otherwise exist between domestic and foreign investments. That is, the domestic corporate tax must be applied on a current basis to the investor's pro-rata share of corporate profits (as the Carter Commission originally recommended, for example), and the foreign corporation tax must be fully credited. Further, any withholding tax on dividends should also be fully credited against domestic personal income tax. In practice, however, individual portfolio investors normally can claim credit only for foreign withholding tax against domestic personal income tax liability.

Table 4.2 sets out the possibilities for both individual and corporate portfolio investors under the present American and Canadian tax systems.[10] Case 2 is an American investor in Canada, and Case 3 a Canadian investor in the United States.

When the source country has a dividend credit system, as does Canada, capital-export neutrality requires that a residence country with a separate entity system (like the United States) would have to levy a special tax to absorb the benefits of the dividend credit extended by the source country to nonresident investors.[11] If this is not done, foreign investment is unduly encouraged to the extent that net yields on foreign shares are increased by the dividend credit (unless, of course, the increase is fully capitalized into higher stock prices—a possibly significant qualification which cannot be discussed further here).

The difficulties in achieving capital-export neutrality are greater when the capital-exporting country employs any other system of taxing corporate-source income than a separate entity system. For example, if the capital-exporting country also has a dividend credit system, what is required for neutrality really amounts to integration of the *foreign* corporate tax with domestic income tax. Full domestic dividend credit must be extended to Canadian shareholders in foreign corporations in order to place them in the same tax position as shareholders in those corporations which only operate domestically.

If corporate investment decisions are assumed to be affected only by taxes at the corporate level, it might be argued that there is no need to grant such a credit to shareholders in foreign corporations. But if this policy is followed and the payout ratio of foreign corporations has to be increased to compensate for the failure to grant the dividend credit to their shareholders, the result is non-neutral treatment of investment at home and abroad. Since the potential revenue loss from this system if the source country levies a high corporate tax appears to constitute an effective bar to its implementation in practice, full neutrality in this respect seems unattainable.

Table 4.2
Tax Arrangements Needed in Capital-Exporting Country
to Achieve Capital-Export Neutrality
for Portfolio Investment

Capital-Exporter	Capital-Importer	
	Separate Corporate Tax	Dividend Credit
Separate Corporate Tax	Case 1	Case 2
Dividend Credit	Case 3	Case 4

Requirements for Neutrality:

Case 1   Current corporate tax is applied to pro rata profits with full credit (including refunds if necessary) for foreign corporate and withholding taxes.   In case of an individual investor, personal income tax is applied to dividends with full gross-up and credit for foreign withholding tax.

Case 2   As for Case 1. Note that if a foreign dividend credit is extended, a special recoupment tax must be levied to restore neutrality.

Case 3   As for Case 1, with no additional tax imposed on subsequent distribution and shareholders given full domestic dividend credit.

Case 4   As for Case 3, subject to the qualification in Case 2.

Furthermore, in principal no additional tax—such as the French *precompte* or the British advance corporation tax—should be imposed to compensate for a dividend credit granted to dividends paid out of foreign profits. In this respect at least, Canada's treatment of its investors abroad is more neutral (less nationalistic!) than that of these countries, owing to the virtually unique Canadian practice of granting dividend credits whether or not domestic tax has been paid on the underlying corporate income.[12]

These difficulties in achieving international tax neutrality are exacerbated if the source country also has some sort of integration system, as has the United Kingdom and as was recently discussed in the United States, for example. If both countries have comparable levels of corporate tax as well as distribution relief which is extended to foreign portfolio investors, however, the problems can largely be avoided. What has been labelled "effective reciprocity" (Sato and Bird, 1975) will then be achieved, as will capital-export neutrality.

In short, any form of integration between corporate and personal income taxes introduces some difficulties and complexities into the tax arrangements required to achieve capital-export neutrality. Relief at the shareholder level (dividend credit system) raises the question of the integration of the foreign corporate tax with the domestic personal income tax at either the corporate or personal level. This is more difficult when the partner country does not provide similar relief (the United States) than when it does (the United Kingdom). On the other hand, the extension of the dividend credit to foreign investors, rather than helping to achieve capital-export neutrality as one might at first think—and as the United States has frequently argued—actually requires that offsetting measures be adopted by the partner country if neutrality is to be achieved. If course, if the foreign jurisdiction does not act to restore neutrality, the result will be to favour investment abroad by its residents over domestic investment.

Any integration between corporate and personal taxes thus makes the achievement of capital-export neutrality more difficult than when corporations are taxed separately from the personal income tax. The weight to be attached to this finding largely depends, of course, on the importance attached to achieving international economic efficiency in the design of national policy.

Corporate-Personal Tax Integration and National Welfare Maximization

What seems more likely to be important in the real world is for tax policy to be guided by a quite different perspective on efficiency, adopting a criterion concerned with the allocation of resources from a purely *national* viewpoint in contrast to the world viewpoint underlying the objective of capital-export neutrality. To ensure the efficient allocation of resources from a strictly national viewpoint, as noted earlier, the gross return on domestic investment must be compared with the net (after-foreign-tax) return on foreign investment. If there were no other costs or benefits of foreign investment, national advantage would be maximized by equating this gross return with the net (after-tax) return from foreign investment, a result which could be achieved by applying the *deduction* approach to foreign taxes. Essentially, this is what Canada already does for foreign taxes in excess of the credit limit, as discussed below.

This procedure would also achieve "national equity" among individual taxpayers in the sense of treating them the same with respect to income received in the country of residence.[13] To the extent that foreign investment is a complement to, rather than a substitute for, domestic investment, these results would, of course, have to be modified. This point emphasizes again the importance of distinguishing between portfolio and direct investment since, while direct investment abroad may be (at least sometimes) complementary to investment at home, portfolio investment abroad is clearly a substitute for portfolio investment at home.

Assume, for example, that the gross profits from a domestic and a foreign investment are each equal to 100 and that the tax rate in both countries is 50 percent. If the full credit approach is employed, investors would continue to invest abroad until the *gross* profits from foreign investment are equal to those on domestic investment. National gains from this investment, however, will be reduced by the foreign tax to 50. If, instead, the deduction approach is applied, foreign investment will become less profitable than domestic investment, since the investor will now have to pay 50 in foreign tax and 25 in domestic tax. The gross profit on foreign investment would in these circumstances have to be 200 to yield the same net profit to the investor as would 100 in gross domestic profits. National gains on foreign investment (profits net of foreign tax) would then be equal to total gains on domestic investment. The foreign tax rate then becomes crucial on location decisions because the *net* profits on foreign investment have to be equated with the *gross* profits on domestic investment. Encouragement of investment in low-tax countries and discouragement in high-tax countries will thus result from the deduction method (as from the exemption method, or territorial principle) which is, of course, one of the intended results of the national efficiency criterion.

The difficulties arising from the integration of corporate and personal taxes are, however, less serious in this case than in the international efficiency case. The problem of integrating foreign corporate tax with domestic personal income tax, for instance, ceases to exist, because under this criterion foreign investment should bear at least the same domestic corporate tax as domestic investment. A dividend credit would, however, still have to be given to distributions to resident shareholders of foreign income if corporate investment policy is assumed to be influenced by the cumulated tax burdens of shareholders, because otherwise foreign investment would be unduly penalized and national gains would not be maximized.[14]

Complex as it may appear, this brief discussion provides only a preliminary sketch of the steps that would be needed to develop a fully "neutral" system of taxing portfolio investment from the point of view of either allocative efficiency in general or the pursuit of national interests more narrowly defined. Incomplete as it is, however, this discussion serves to suggest that the present Canadian system of taxing such investment (discussed below) is not neutral. Moreover, given the differing systems of corporate taxation in other countries, it is not possible to devise a completely neutral and uniform system. Partly for this reason, an important feature of the taxation of international income flows is the network of bilateral tax treaties that serves to accommodate such special features of different countries.

5.

Attaining Neutrality: Tax Treaties[15]

Three important considerations underlie the negotiation of bilateral tax treaties. These are, respectively, the *allocative*, *distributive*, and what may be termed the *restrictive* functions of such international agreements, each of which enshrines elements of compromise struck in particular economic and political circumstances.

Allocative Considerations

Tax treaties between industrial countries usually address a variety of specific bilateral fiscal issues that ultimately determine the effective rate of tax on non-resident income. Included are definitions of accounting components of income, the structure and level of rates of direct taxes on foreign-source income, the form of foreign tax relief, the commitment (or otherwise) to principles of national treatment and non-discrimination, and the degree to which tax preferences are extended to non-residents.

The clauses and conditions pertinent to foreign portfolio investment are a small, although often economically significant, subset of the terms of a tax treaty. In this respect, the first focus of mutual concern has generally been to increase the efficiency of the international allocation of capital. This treaty objective is sometimes referred to as "elimination of double taxation" but, in principle, it is broader than that. The aim is to coordinate national tax systems so that taxation in one country or another does not sway decisions to invest at home versus abroad. The objective is thus tax neutrality with respect to international investment. With respect to portfolio investment, this objective has led to the primacy of residence country taxation and the restriction of source country taxation through the imposition of maximum limits on withholding taxes, especially on interest paid abroad. Clearly, however, to the extent any nation is intent on unilaterally maximizing its own national welfare by maintaining taxes that generate gains for itself at the expense of its neighbours—through, for example, terms-of-trade effects—the incentive for mutually advantageous treaty negotiation is lessened.

In the international setting the economic cost of taxation—or excess burden—is the loss of aggregate output due to distortionary national policies. Misallocation of resources results internationally from both fiscal barriers to trade and restrictions on international factor movements. By reducing the latter, tax treaties are designed to move overlapping tax systems closer to neutrality, to reduce international excess burden, and to increase economic efficiency. Countries may, of course, impose taxes that induce inefficiencies. At best, a tax treaty may seek to ensure that in spite of such national tax distortions the interaction of the national tax systems does not further distort investors' choice between investing at home or abroad.

Distributive Considerations

A second major issue in international tax negotiation concerns the sharing, between capital-exporting and capital-importing countries, of tax revenue from foreign investment. It is inevitable when dealing with concepts such as distributional equity that the analytic basis is more value-laden and arbitrary than that used for dealing with questions of allocative efficiency.[16] As a practical matter, however, problems of allocation of international nvestiment and the distribution of returns from international investment, including tax revenue, cannot really be separated. As shown in Chapters 2 and 4, tax arrangements that achieve a particular degree of allocative efficiency simultaneously determine a corresponding international distribution of fiscal revenue.

If two countries export capital to each other, tax distortions are minimized all-round—the international perspective—if each adopts either the credit or (if rates are equal) the exemption method. In fact, tax treaties usually include a reciprocal arrangement of one or the other methods for every category of foreign-source income. By adopting the foreign tax credit the capital-exporting country acknowledges the capital-importing country's first tax claim on earnings of capital, including foreign-owned capital, in its jurisdiction. Indeed, capital-importing countries typically take a large bite and, as long as their taxes are credited against a liability in the capital-exporting country, they can capture tax revenue with no marginal allocative consequences. The bilateral distribution of tax revenue from foreign investment approaches equality if stocks of foreign investment are equally distributed and if, in each country, tax rates are approximately the same. This more or less automatic result of equal fiscal shares between equally placed countries helps explain why the network of tax treaties among industrialized countries, which is essentially a series of bilateral agreements, has overtones of a multilateral tax convention.[17] Since the converse of the equality condition is also true, however, the inevitable distributional imbalance is responsible for relatively slow progress in treaty negotiations between rich and poor countries or other pairs of countries unequally placed.[18] The United States, in particular, has a much less extensive network of tax treaties with developing nations than is the case for Canada, Britain, and most Western European nations.

The protracted negotiations for a new tax treaty between Canada and the United States, which began in 1971 to replace the 1942 treaty, further illustrate the difficulty of difference. Since American investment in Canada is substantially greater than investment the other way round, Canada stood to lose tax revenue from equal reciprocal reductions in withholding tax rates or from a shift in emphasis, within any income category, from taxation based on the source of income to taxation based on the residence of taxpayer. The United States wanted the lower rates of withholding tax called for in the OECD Model Treaty, which proposed a maximum 10 percent withholding tax rate on interest and 5 percent on dividends.[19] Canada stood firm in its resolve for higher rates and was especially insistent that the rate on dividends be the same as the rate on interest. The Canadian position was influenced both by the fact that dividend flows out of Canada are higher than dividend flows to Canada and by the general policy of encouraging broader ownership of Canadian business. For similar reasons Canada also earlier considered it necessary to enter reservations on the OECD draft convention, which reflects the attitudes of its principal authors, the United States, Germany, France, and the United Kingdom, all capital-exporting nations in favour of lower taxes on portfolio investment in the country of source and unrestricted taxation in the country of residence.

Tax treaties typically include clauses regarding nondiscriminatory tax treatment of foreign and domestic capital. In practice, equal treatment, sometimes called "national treatment", is achieved if all capital within each nation is taxed by the same domestically specified rules and rates. An international agreement between countries A and B to extend national treatment to foreign capital obviously does *not* require that the structure or rates of capital taxation be the same in A and B. Specific features of domestic tax systems are generally kept off treaty agenda to avoid encroaching on domestic fiscal sovereignty. This approach is also consistent with a widely held international tax convention regarding overlapping tax jurisdictions: the priority to tax is source country first, residence country second. Accordingly, treaties generally focus on withholding tax rates on interest, dividends, and other earnings on foreign capital because such taxes are levied at the border and are thus, by definition, discriminatory. This focus, of course, also accords with the interests of capital-exporting nations in reducing source-country taxation of returns on portfolio investment.

An Agreed Set of Rules

A third purpose of tax treaties, after the allocative and distributive functions, is to establish a degree of fiscal stability in the environment in which international investment takes place. The fact that national tax jurisdictions are in principle limitless, coupled with indisputable national sovereignty in internal tax matters affecting individual nations, creates a situation in which destructive international conflict or capricious manoeuvring may arise. Tax treaties establish formal compromise in areas of potential international jurisdictional conflict involving taxation. Furthermore, provisions for review and renegotiation of tax treaties help reconcile unforeseen problems as they arise.

Investors shy away from uncertainty. Tax administrators, likewise, want security in tax administration. As a formal agreement between nations, a tax treaty spells out the rules of the game for all the players, investors and nations alike. Entrepreneurial risks that might otherwise exist in the absence of constraints on aggregate taxation of foreign-source income are thus reduced or eliminated. Risks involving tax administration are also reduced both in terms of the narrow definition of risk involving revenue and in the broader perspective in which taxation is a dimension of policy determining national gains from international trade and investment.

Because tax uncertainty lowers a barrier to international investment, the "restrictive" function of a tax treaty is consistent with the "allocative" function. Eliminating the risk of international tax uncertainty is a necessary condition, although not a sufficient condition, for the efficient international allocation of capital.

For tax administrators, the explicit terms of a treaty facilitate international tax administration. In particular, the interaction of two governments dealing with one tax base may help solve administrative problems beyond the scope of any one government alone. Tax treaties generally provide a legal mechanism for exchange of information, including in some cases simultaneous tax audits of firms operating trans-nationally in order to ensure compliance and to minimize evasion. Although relatively little use has been made in the past of such international information flows, the growing integration of the world capital market has led recently to serious consideration by the Organization for Economic Cooperation and Development of the means to facilitate information exchange between tax administrations (OECD, 1987).

No tax treaty can possibly deal with all potential difficulties, so most modern treaties contain *competent authority* clauses which allow issues to be addressed on an *ad hoc* basis insofar as they cannot be resolved by explicit terms of the treaty. The most frequent and difficult matters pertain to interpreting so-called "source rules" which define the allocation of income between source and residence countries. In dealing with these problems, the competent authority mechanism in principle assures the taxpayer of all intended benefits of a tax treaty. Since treaty cases encompass an interplay of distinctly different systems, the competent authorities in practice have generally followed a flexible and pragmatic approach, taking into account various tax laws in the countries involved and differences in accounting practices as well as alternative points of view in treaty interpretation.

The goal of providing relief to the international taxpayer has thus been accomplished in part by international tax agreements which preserve each country's fiscal sovereignty and accommodate differences on a reasonable basis. The same goal has also been pursued by unilateral national policies described in Chapter 4. On the whole it seems fair to say that the combination of both approaches has achieved fairly equitable and efficient results at least between industrial countries with relatively balanced capital flows and well-run tax administrations. However, the same modern technology that underlies the development of the sophisticated world capital market has led to the flourishing of tax havens and extreme exploitation of small tax differences between countries. Consequently, major problems have emerged in recent years in ensuring the adequate enforcement of taxes on international income flows. It remains to be seen whether these new pressures can be accommodated by further adjustments in the existing unilateral and bilateral "neutrality" mechanisms or whether they will, in the end, result in more major changes in the international tax order—perhaps the emergence of a new international tax enforcement agency (Intertax!) or perhaps the effective abolition of taxes on capital income in general (Bird 1988).

6.

Canadian Taxation of Portfolio Investment

Although, as noted earlier, there are substantial differences between portfolio and direct investment, two fundamental questions arise regarding national tax policy toward *all* foreign investment. First, is the existing tax structure responsible for "distortions" in the international allocation of capital? That is, is a capital-import or capital-export bias created by the interaction of the national tax structure and tax structures abroad? Secondly, how sensitive is foreign investment (and related policy variables, including tax revenues) to changes in national tax treatment of the earnings of foreign investment? While the answers to the second question are inherently empirical and hence beyond the scope of this paper, the first question can largely be answered in theoretical terms.

The general intent of current Canadian tax policy with respect to foreign-source income appears to be to recognize and incorporate the economic distinction between portfolio and direct investment and generally to promote capital-export neutrality with respect to direct investment while minimizing unnecessary tax revenue loss through foreign portfolio investment. This approach seems consistent with the following perception of

63

Canada's situation in the world. First, Canada is a major net importer of capital, and this source of foreign savings is considered to be essential to continued economic growth. Second, Canadian corporations are assumed to have worthwhile direct investment opportunities abroad which, if exploited, will have potential feedback effects on the Canadian economy. In other words, foreign direct investment is apparently considered to be largely *complementary* to Canadian domestic investment. Third, Canadian foreign portfolio investment is unambiguously a *substitute* for portfolio investment in Canada, and may perhaps be placed outside Canada at least in part to avoid Canadian tax. Finally, Canadian corporations are frequently involved in both foreign direct and portfolio investments and the line between them is not always easy to draw.

Whatever the empirical merits of each step in this argument—and they are for the most part far from clear—on the whole current policy only makes sense if one accepts each of these propositions, namely, that capital import is essential, that direct capital export is good, that portfolio capital export is bad, and that it is hard to tell the difference between good and bad outflows. The remainder of this section briefly summarizes the relevant Canadian rules on the taxation of foreign-source income.[20]

Portfolio investment income—interest and dividends—is included in income in Canada when received (that is, in effect it is taxed on a current rather than deferred basis). The recipient is permitted to claim a credit for foreign taxes paid in computing the federal tax liability and, in certain instances, in calculating the provincial liability as well. The foreign tax credit, however, is restricted to 15 percent of the gross amount of any foreign income. To the extent that the foreign tax exceeds this figure, it may be deducted in computing taxable income.

Portfolio Investment of Individuals

In practice, foreign-source interest income received by Canadian individuals—typically derived from bank deposits, bonds, or other fixed income securities—is often either completely untaxed at source or, at most, incurs a relatively low withholding tax. Many United States-source interest payments to Canada, for instance, are not taxed, so that there is no question of claiming a foreign tax credit. Moreover, a substantial and perhaps majority share of foreign portfolio investment of Canadians is held by effectively tax-exempt entities such as pension funds.

Foreign-source dividend income received by taxable Canadian individuals, on the other hand, is more likely to have been taxed at source as well as through a withholding tax. In this case, although a tax credit will usually be claimed, the limitation of the foreign tax credit to 15 percent of foreign gross income obviously creates some potential for "double taxation" of foreign-source dividends received by Canadian shareholders. The resulting bias against (equity) portfolio capital export is further heightened through the tax preference for investing in Canadian equity securities resulting from the dividend tax credit granted on domestic shares to resident shareholders. The resulting downward pressure on pre-tax yields on Canadian equities relative to foreign equities implies that Canadian tax policy on balance not only discourages portfolio capital exports from Canada but also indirectly discourages portfolio capital imports—foreign purchases of Canadian equities—as well.[21] Even if only slightly, tax factors thus appear likely to play at least some inhibiting role against both private capital inflows and outflows.

The extent to which international portfolio capital is actually diverted by this tax bias, of course, is an empirical question. Since more than 90 percent of equity securities are held by corporate financial institutions, less than 10 percent remains to be influenced by the tax factors just described as pertinent to individuals. Moreover, to the extent a large share of the portfolio holdings of Canadian individuals is traditionally held in Canadian equities anyway, this small international tax bias seems rather unlikely to exert a substantial effect on the overall domestic:foreign mix of portfolio holdings by Canadian individual investors.

Corporate Portfolio Investment

With respect to the foreign-source earnings of subsidiaries of Canadian corporations, Canadian tax law is structured to distinguish portfolio investment with virtually no entrepreneurial involvement from that in which a Canadian resident has a substantial financial commitment, albeit short of a controlling interest.[22]

This distinction is achieved by defining a "foreign affiliate" as a non-resident corporation in which the equity percentage of a taxpayer resident in Canada is at least 10 percent. The taxpayer is generally understood to be a Canadian *corporate* taxpayer; the foreign-source income is typically in the form of dividends paid by a foreign affiliate to a Canadian parent company. If the foreign holding is less than 10 percent, dividends from the foreign source are fully taxable by Canada in the hands of the Canadian corporate portfolio investor. Immediately we see a bias in Canadian corporate portfolio holdings comparable to the bias outlined above in terms of individuals and the Canadian dividend tax credit available to them. Such dividends received by one Canadian corporation from another are generally tax-exempt while dividends received by a Canadian corporation from a foreign portfolio investment are taxable in Canada, there is significant incentive for Canadian corporations to favour investment in other Canadian corporations.

At a higher level of control, involving a distinction between portfolio investment and direct investment, a "controlled foreign affiliate" is one which is not only a foreign affiliate in the "10 percent sense" but also one in which the Canadian controlling resident must also have the absolute right to elect a majority of the directors of the controlled affiliate if, indeed, it is not owned outright.[23]

Canadian taxation of offshore income of Canadians has adopted a hands-off "territorial approach" to income from direct investment and a "residence approach"—a worldwide claim—to the rest. The foreign affiliate rule, and the distinctions that it entails, are part of a structure to prevent abuse of an inherent weakness in the dichotomous approach. Such abuse, for example, would occur if offshore income of various kinds is channeled to a majority-owned subsidiary that in turn forwards the collective income to the Canadian parent as dividends free of Canadian tax. There is a need to identify the original sources of income flowing through a nonresident intermediary, to disentangle the dividend flow to Canada into strands of active business income and passive, property, or portfolio income. In simplest terms, income ultimately derived from the active operations of direct investments is dubbed tax-exempt surplus which, as the name implies, is categorically exempt from Canadian tax. On the other hand, income that is not active business income is taxed in Canada either on a *deferral* basis, that is, as received in Canada, which is the case for individuals and other-than-controlled foreign affiliates, or on a *current* basis if it is earned by controlled foreign affiliates. The income distinction is not consistent with conventional definitions in consolidation accounting and thus Canada has devised a unique system to circumscribe Foreign Accrual Property Income (FAPI).

Foreign Accrual Property Income

In addition to the three-way categorization of the nature of foreign investment—(1) portfolio (less than 10 percent), (2) foreign affiliate (greater than 10 percent), and (3) controlled foreign affiliate (10 percent plus "control")—Canadian tax law further specifies a three-way breakdown of foreign-source income, although not in exact correspondence to these investment categories: portfolio dividends and interest are distinguished from foreign accrual property income (FAPI) and, in turn, FAPI is distinguished from the "active business income" of foreign affiliates. Portfolio income, as noted above, is taxed on a current basis with a limited credit while active business income is generally not subject to tax in Canada. FAPI receives special, complex treatment basically intended to discourage avoidance of Canadian tax through offshore operations by piercing the corporate veil and treating "tax haven" operations as though they were branches, that is taxing their income on a current basis.[24]

FAPI consists, in principle, of income from other than *active* business abroad. It is essentially a foreign affiliate's *passive* or investment income, including capital gains, interest and dividends. In this context of offshore portfolio income, interaffiliate dividends received by a foreign affiliate are excluded from its FAPI, however, because such dividends would have been previously taxed as FAPI of the dividend-paying affiliate, if in fact the dividend is paid out of FAPI. To state the general case, interaffiliate dividends are not FAPI because the tax characteristics of the related underlying income of the payor (whether active income of FAPI) have been determined and dealt with in the surplus accounts of the payor affiliate.[25]

"Tracing" is thus required to apply the FAPI rules, and difficulties may arise, for example, if such dividends are subject to foreign withholding tax. Since FAPI is fully taxed on a current basis in Canada in the year in which it arises and subsequent dividends out of FAPI are excluded from income, a complex basis for crediting foreign withholding taxes on dividends has been devised, essentially tracing back through the international inter-affiliate structure to match income, withholding taxes, and allowable foreign tax credits in Canada.[26] Dividends received by foreign affiliates from Canadian corporates are excluded from FAPI of a controlled foreign affiliate of a Canadian corporation because such dividends would have been tax exempt if received by the Canadian corporation directly.

On the other hand, in some circumstances income from services that would otherwise be considered active business income may be included in an affiliate's FAPI, for example, where the affiliate makes a charge for services that is deductible in computing the income from a business carried on in Canada by any person who controls or is a member of the controlling group of the affiliate or who is related to such a person. This provision is obviously intended to remove any tax advantage from using a subsidiary of a Canadian corporation in a low-tax jurisdiction to provide services to its parent because the profit from such a service operation that would otherwise be diverted to the subsidiary will be included, through the FAPI rules, in the income of the parent. Indeed, in general, as noted above, the FAPI provisions are designed to prevent Canadian residents from either avoiding or postponing current Canadian tax on certain "passive" (invest-ment) income which could otherwise be diverted with relative ease to foreign corporations or trusts. The FAPI rules are intended to bring total current taxes, Canadian and foreign, on such income up to the effective Canadian rates.

When FAPI is included in a Canadian taxpayer's income, the taxpayer is entitled to claim a deduction for certain foreign taxes, known as "foreign accrual taxes", that became payable in the year the FAPI is recognized *or* in any of the five following years, thus necessitating a complex tracing system. The foreign accrual tax is grossed up by what is called the "relevant tax factor" (2 for an individual or, for a corporation, the reciprocal of the corporate tax), thereby giving the deduction much the same impact as a direct credit for foreign tax against Canadian tax. The purpose of this gross-up and deduction system is to exclude from the Canadian resident's income any portion of the FAPI on which the equivalent of Canadian tax has been paid abroad. If intra-corporate dividends pass through more than one tier of controlled foreign affiliate, no deduction is allowed for foreign taxes beyond the first affiliate to receive dividends; there is no flow-through provision. As noted above, this provision may be potentially troublesome for Canadian multinationals with more than two tiers abroad including, for example, a holding company in a tax haven, but such arrangements, of course, are what the FAPI rules were originally designed to keep in check. However, since taxed FAPI becomes taxable surplus, the related underlying tax account of the upper-tier affiliates will include taxes subsequently imposed. In practice, with proper planning it is generally possible to achieve effective relief of such taxes.

The rules for the taxation of dividends received by Canadian corporations from abroad are complex, but the result is that active business income in a treaty country is exempt from Canadian tax—in effect the territorial principle is applied—while similar income in a non-treaty country[27] is taxed on a deferral basis, that is, as repatriated, with a foreign tax credit being allowed. FAPI, and branch income, on the other hand, are taxed on a current basis, again with a credit (though limited in some cases), and basically the same treatment is extended to portfolio investment.

This system of taxing foreign-source income—among the most complex parts of the entire Canadian income tax system[28]—originated in concern for the possibility of tax avoidance by sophisticated taxpayers through the use of various foreign tax havens on the one hand, and the practical impossibility of monitoring foreign financial flows abroad on the other. The principal precedent for Canada's FAPI rules was Subpart F of the United States Internal Revenue Code, introduced in 1962. As in the American case, the presumption apparently is that it is in Canada's interest to remove the advantages of investing through tax havens; and also as in the American case, it is far from clear how successful the measures intended to achieve this goal have actually been.[29]

The fact that very little tax appears to be collected on FAPI may reflect the successful discouragement of the practices at which these complex rules were aimed. Or it may, as some practitioners suggest, reflect rather the success with which they have been able to avoid having FAPI brought into the tax system. In the absence of a close study of individual taxpayers—and perhaps even with such a study—it is very hard to tell what the effect of these rules has been.[30]

There is also some question of the depth of Canadian resolve on these matters. In 1975, prompted primarily by concern for the sagging fortunes of Massey Ferguson, the Canadian tax authorities introduced a significant change in the definition of active versus passive foreign source income. The change in definition, essentially relaxing the rules and broadening the base of exempt-surplus income, had an immediate and substantial influence on how Canadian multinational enterprises arranged their international finance. The change concerned the categorization of intra-firm transfers, that is transactions between subsidiaries of a firm. Previously, receipts for intra-firm loans, management fees, or similar items had been defined as property income of the receiving subsidiary. However, with the change, such receipts became active business income and, as a result, the income was tax-exempt surplus in Canada. The new definition gave rise to such notorious arrangements as "The Double Dip" whereby the interest deduction on Canadian-sourced funds is taken both in Canada and, say, the United States with the interest flow from the latter accumulating in a financial subsidiary in a tax haven, eventually returning to Canada as exempt surplus. With the Double Dip, the after-tax cost of debt capital for foreign investment is close to zero.[31]

On the whole, it seems unlikely that the complex rules governing Canadian corporate portfolio investment have much practical effect in terms of their original purpose of classifying and treating separately various categories of offshore income. Almost all business income of foreign subsidiaries qualifies in practice as "exempt surplus" and can thus be brought home free of Canadian tax. Most of the balance can, with proper planning, be repatriated as preferentially-taxed capital gains (although that preference is being eliminated). By the use of third-country conduit corporations, foreign withholding taxes can be lowered. And so on. In short, Canadian investors abroad have so many international tax planning opportunities despite FAPI and other complexities that experienced practitioners have been known to refer to Canadian taxation of foreign-source income as a "voluntary tax". Few taxpayers get enmeshed in these complexities and those that do are, it appears, usually well-enough advised to escape relatively unscathed.

The result in practice may thus be to mitigate the bias against foreign portfolio investment and to strengthen the bias for foreign direct investment that appear inherent in the structure of the system itself. The former result may be efficient in world (if not national) terms but the latter seems likely to be inefficient from both national and world perspectives, although again it would need a careful empirical study to determine whether this bias has a significant influence on investment patterns. As a first step towards such a study, the next two chapters explore a little further the probable direction and nature of tax biases on capital flows in theoretical terms.

7.

Taxation and 'Abnormal' International Capital Flows[32]

What is Normal?

International capital, according to the traditional theory set out earlier, will flow from a country in which the rate of return is relatively low to one where the return is relatively higher. The principle holds in the presence of taxation as long as domestic and foreign-source returns are subject to the same effective tax rate, thus establishing capital export neutrality. The principle holds even if the two countries have different effective rates of tax on interest income. As long as policies to promote capital-export neutrality are maintained, equilibrium capital allocation is characterized by international equality of pre-tax returns and domestic:foreign equality of after-tax returns for investors in the capital-exporting nation (although private after-tax returns are not necessarily internationally equal). Subsequent changes in relative returns cause capital to flow in the normal direction.

On the other hand, a capital flow may be termed "abnormal" if it is not in the direction dictated by the prevailing international return differential. If capital does not flow from the low to the high return country, the situation reflects some sort of market intervention or barrier to international capital flows.

There are two possible abnormal types of capital flows to consider: first, simultaneous investment in domestic markets and, second, simultaneous investment in foreign markets. Since both of these curiosities are frequently observed in the real world, it is obvious that the international yield differential alone is not sufficient to explain the direction of international portfolio capital flows. The purpose of this chapter is to explain how taxation may induce such irregularities and to outline the policy implications of the phenomenon for an open economy.

Root Causes of Anomalous Capital Flows

In practice, the relevant return on an investment denominated in a foreign currency is more complex than the simple interest yield on the foreign security. Since changes in the exchange rate impose foreign exchange gains and losses, the full return on a security denominated in a foreign currency is the sum of two distinct components of yield, the interest rate and the foreign exchange gain or loss. Indeed, to the extent that there are no distortions or impediments to the flow of capital, equilibrium in international capital markets is established when, between pairs of countries, the interest rate in one country equals the interest rate in the other country plus the expected annual rate of change of the exchange rate.

A potentially important distortion in international capital markets arises when interest and foreign exchange gains are taxed differently from each other. The problem is compounded when (as is generally the case between definitions, rules, and rates differ between countries) interest and foreign exchange gains are taxed differently according to the residence of the investor.

To illustrate, if it is assumed that all foreign-source interest is taxed as income while foreign exchange gains and losses receive preferential tax treatment, then for a domestic investor holding a security denominated in a foreign currency, the after-tax yield on the security will be larger the more the yield consists of foreign exchange gain. Such gains will constitute a larger component of the yield on foreign securities the more the domestic currency is expected to depreciate through the period. Assuming other things to be equal, domestic investors will thus require a smaller pre-tax yield on securities denominated in foreign currency than on investments in the domestic market if the domestic currency is expected to depreciate through the holding period. It follows, then, that when domestic currency sells at a forward discount, there will be a range of pre-tax yields for which the domestic yield *exceeds* the foreign yield yet foreign securities are purchased by domestic investors. The result is a capital outflow in the face of a relatively low yield on foreign securities.

If investors abroad, on the other hand, respond in the standard fashion to the international yield differential, they would invest in the higher yields offered by securities denominated in the depreciating currency and hence export capital to the domestic economy. There would thus simultaneously be capital outflows by domestic investors and capital inflows from investors abroad. This "abnormal" pattern of international capital flows could occur over a range of international yield differentials (domestic yield higher than foreign yield) provided the treatment of capital gains is less preferential for investors abroad than it is for domestic investors. The necessary condition is that investors abroad face a smaller differential than domestic investors in the rates applicable to interest income and foreign exchange gains (losses) respectively, including the archetypal case where foreign exchange gains and losses are treated as part of ordinary income. Since, for example, foreign exchange gains earned on investments held by Americans are treated in the United States as ordinary income for investments of less than six months, this condition may well hold for at least some United States investors holding Canadian bonds.

The structure of tax and international yields could also, under different circumstances, establish an incentive for domestic investors to purchase domestic securities despite higher pre-tax yields abroad. The financial manoeuvring in this situation is somewhat more complex than in the previous case. The trick is for domestic investors to borrow *foreign* funds to buy securities denominated in *domestic* currency. This is an effective strategy if the domestic currency is selling at a forward premium, that is, if the domestic currency is expected to appreciate. In that case, borrowing foreign funds to finance the purchase of domestic securities generates foreign exchange gains on the appreciation of the domestic currency. Assuming these gains are taxed preferentially, on an after-tax basis they can more than compensate for the higher foreign borrowing costs. Every dollar lost through higher interest expense represents an after-tax cost of $(1- income tax rate) when deducted from other income. Every dollar of domestic dollar premium, on the other hand, represents an expected gain of $(1- capital gains tax rate). There will thus be a range of foreign and domestic yields in which the foreign yield is higher but which is nevertheless consistent with purchases of domestic securities by domestic investors.

In an empirical study of abnormal international capital flows, Levi (1977) identified numerous occasions in which the direction of after-tax profitable international investment as between Canada and the United States was *not* the direction suggested by the pre-tax differential in yield, thus lending support to the argument summarized above.

When withholding taxes are not fully offset by the foreign tax credit—which, as explained in Chapter 3, is often the case on international portfolio investment—there is in fact a *wider* range of international yield differentials over which simultaneous domestic purchases of domestic securities could occur. The point is consistent with the earlier discussion of the investment effects of a withholding tax in a "small" country like Canada. The withholding tax drives a wedge between foreign and Canadian pre-tax yield, forcing the latter to be greater than the former by a factor of $1/(1 - t)$. This in itself induces domestic investment in Canadian securities by Canadians and simultaneously reduces the equilibrium flow of foreign capital. Therefore, when unequal differentials in interest income and capital gains taxes serve to discourage international capital flows—as in the case of simultaneous domestic purchases—a withholding tax heightens the barriers.

Barriers by Design for Interest Rate Independence

There is an interesting implication of this analysis for a problem Canada faces with respect to interest rates. As a small country which in principle is committed to flexible exchange rates, Canada is usually assumed to be unable to pursue an independent interest rate policy because reductions in domestic interest rates induce capital outflows which depress the value of the Canadian dollar at a rate which offsets the Canadian:foreign nominal interest differential. In turn, the Canadian dollar depreciation leads to a subsequent round of domestic inflation which, to complete the circle, becomes built into even higher interest rates. The only apparent alternative, if the fall in the dollar is to be stemmed when interest rates are lowered, is a regime of capital export controls, which would obviously introduce a whole new set of problems.

If the pattern of international capital flows is not that predicted by *pre-tax* interest rate differentials, however, the apparent abnormal state of affairs cannot, as shown above, be construed as a state of disequilibrium in international capital markets, since equilibrium is really determined with respect to the international set of *after-tax* returns. Since the presumed efficiency of these markets means that capital flows, for all practical purposes, are always in equilibrium, so-called "abnormal" capital flows are really the result of international market responses to after-tax incentives which, under certain circumstances, establish what are tantamount to barriers to international capital.

Even if the pattern of flows does not appear to be abnormal, the tax barriers are, of course, still there. All that has happened is that the configuration of international interest differentials and the forward premium or discount on foreign exchange are such as to provide sufficient after-tax incentive to overcome these barriers.

In addition to withholding taxes, another way to raise such barriers to capital flows would obviously be to impose a tax on transactions involving foreign exchange. Such a tax reduces the after-tax return from investing abroad or from undertaking any transaction involving foreign exchange, including the financial manoeuvring required to arbitrage international interest rate differentials. A tax on foreign exchange transactions, coordinated with domestic interest rate policy, may thus in principle provide a potential means to counter the nemesis of independent interest rate policies, the problem of capital flight, by explicitly creating barriers similar to those responsible for the abnormal capital flows outlined above. Moreover, the range of lower-than-foreign domestic interest rates over which domestic investors will shun foreign investments would no longer be an accidental result of the international interaction of national tax policies. Instead, the range could be determined by policy and could be widened or narrowed by raising or lowering the tax on foreign exchange transactions.

Such a tax is, in a sense, a variable capital export control and hence, of course, involves a move away from the principle of flexible exchange rates.[33] Indeed, a prohibitive rate of tax would amount to an outright restriction of transactions in foreign currencies. Short of this extreme, however, a tax on foreign exchange transactions may be a potentially valuable instrument of policy, by allowing a small country to lower its domestic interest rate while at the same time providing some scope to control the otherwise inevitable hemorrhage of capital and fall in the exchange rate. Domestic investors who, for one reason or another, judge that a deal involving foreign exchange is worthwhile despite the tax, will be free to proceed, but will have to pay for the privilege.

A tax on foreign exchange transactions would be somewhat similar to the Interest Equalization Tax introduced in the United States in 1963 to reduce the outflow of capital. Investments in Canadian securities were, after some fuss, exempted from the tax.[34] However, since a tax on foreign exchange transactions would have a narrower focus than the American tax, it would likely be easier to administer. For one thing, a foreign exchange tax would not require that all foreign investments be recorded or that rules be established for defining return on foreign investment. Moreover, the tax could be administered via the domestic and Canadian international banking system through which virtually all foreign exchange transactions flow. No doubt other channels (or short-circuits) would emerge under such controls, but for a small country like Canada whose currency is not a major international trading currency, most adjustments would involve once-only substitutions of other currencies for the Canadian dollar by those who speculate in foreign exchange. In other words, speculators, insofar as they deal in the Canadian dollar, would be partially pushed out of business. Taxes on international capital flows could perhaps be used constructively in these ways to loosen some of the constraints on policy in an open economy. Since this conclusion is so markedly different from the usual argument that a small country cannot effectively levy a tax on international capital flows without harming its own economy, it may be worth investigating this idea further, both theoretically and empirically, in a country like Canada which would, it appears, like to have more independence of its domestic interest rate from the world rate.

8.

Taxation, Inflation and International Capital Flows

This chapter examines briefly the interaction of inflation, taxation, and interest rates, focusing in particular on implications for the capital stock of an open economy. Inflation in one country relative to inflation abroad may induce international capital movements. This issue is obviously important in a world characterized economically by variance across national rates of inflation and institutionally by capital markets that respond rapidly to international differentials in real after-tax yields.

Inflation affects the real after-tax yield of both domestic and foreign investment by domestic investors as well as the yield of (foreign) investment by foreign investors. Insofar as the impacts of inflation on these three yields are not equal, after-tax yield differentials are created. Subsequent tax arbitrage results in capital reallocation—international capital flows—and rearrangement of the equilibrium mix of domestic and foreign investment.[35] Under reasonable assumptions of interest rate and exchange rate adjustments, the taxation of nominal interest income causes capital to flow to the country experiencing relatively greater inflation.

The Fisher Equation

The foundation of most models of interest rates, inflation, taxation, and exchange rates is the so-called Fisher Equation (Fisher, 1930) linking nominal yields to real yields and inflation. In a closed economy with no taxation, the nominal or "market" rate of interest equals the sum of the expected real rate of interest and the expected rate of inflation. With zero inflation, real and nominal rates of interest are equal. However, when the expected rate of interest is positive—assuming the real rate of interest is independent of inflation—the nominal interest rate increases point-for-point with inflation.

The "neutrality" of inflation—or the constancy of the real rate of interest—means that lenders and borrowers jointly recognize that the real value of the principal of outstanding loans diminishes at a rate equal to the rate of inflation. As part of the equilibrium nominal interest rate, the inflation component compensates lenders for the erosion of the value of principal in each period. Thus the inflation component of the nominal interest rate in an economic sense is not an income flow but rather a repayment of capital. The imposition of tax on what in fact are capital transfers raises the effective rate of tax on real interest.

Investors' decisions, of course, are made in light of after-tax real yields. when nominal interest rates are subject to tax, each point of inflation in a closed economy requires an increase of more than a point in nominal interest rates in order to maintain after-tax real yields.

These concepts are summarized in the following four definitions of nominal and real interest rates in situations with and without taxation. The nominal interest rate is i, the real interest rate is r, and the rate of inflation is $\dot{P}$. The tax rate t applies to nominal interest:

Nominal Interest, No Tax: $\quad i = r + \dot{P}$ (Fisher Equation) [1]

Real Interest, No Tax: $\quad r = i - \dot{P}$ [2]

Real Interest, Tax $\quad r = i (1 - t) - \dot{P}$ [3]

Nominal Interest, Tax $\quad i = (r + \dot{P}) / (1 - t)$ [4]

A one percentage point increase in expected inflation in a closed economy thus requires a corresponding increase of $1/(1-t)$

percentage points in the nominal market interest rate in order to leave lenders' after-tax real yields unchanged. Furthermore, an increase in the tax rate given the inflation rate—also leads to an increase in the nominal interest rate, in this case by a factor of $(r + \dot{P}) / (1 - t)^2$.

The International Fisher Relation

The relation between nominal and real interest extends to two countries with the Fisher Relation holding in each. Internationally integrated capital markets then bring real interest rates into equality to establish what is termed Fisher Open Parity. Denoting foreign variables with asterisks:

$$i - \dot{P} = i^* - \dot{P} = r = r^* \qquad \text{Fisher Open Parity} \qquad [5]$$

Fisher Open Parity implies that the international inflation differential $(\dot{P} - \dot{P}^*)$ equals the nominal interest differential $(i - i^*)$.

The international inflation differential is ultimately reflected in the rate of change of the exchange rate, thus maintaining the relative purchasing power of the respective currencies. That is:

$$i - i^* = \dot{P} - \dot{P}^* = \dot{S} \qquad\qquad\qquad [6]$$

where $\dot{S}$ is the rate of change of the exchange rate. Home currency appreciates ($\dot{S}$ is positive) when domestic inflation is less than foreign inflation, whereas Home currency depreciates ($\dot{S}$ is negative) when domestic inflation exceeds foreign inflation.

The nominal market rate of interest in an open economy thus equals the nominal interest rate abroad plus the rate of currency appreciation (or depreciation). This relation, termed International Interest Parity, is an equilibrium condition in international capital markets without taxation. Investors are indifferent between domestic and foreign investments—that is, real yields are equal—when the nominal domestic yield equals the nominal foreign yield net of foreign exchange gains or losses.

Taxation and International Interest Parity

Introducing taxation in this framework, a domestic investor taxed equally on domestic and foreign investments is assumed to be indifferent between domestic and foreign investment when real after-tax yields are equal at home and abroad, that is when:

$$i\,(1 - t) - \dot{P} = (i^* - \dot{P}^* + \dot{P})\,(1 - t) - \dot{P} \qquad [7]$$

or simply:

$$i = i^* + \dot{S} \qquad [8]$$

Asterisks again denote foreign variables. The left-hand side is the real after-tax yield on domestic investment. The right-hand side is the real after-tax yield on foreign investment which explicitly includes the rate of change of the foreign exchange rate under the conditions of Fisher Open Parity.

If the tax rate (t_d) levied on domestic investment income is greater than the tax rate (t_f) applied to offshore investment income, as would be true, for example, if foreign investments were sheltered, the result, again with the domestic real after-tax yield on the left and the offshore real after-tax yield on the right, is:

$$i\,(1 - t_d) = (i^* + \dot{S})\,(1 - t_f) \qquad [9]$$

What these equations mean is that in equilibrium when an investor is indifferent between investment at home and abroad, differential taxation of domestic and foreign investment income causes an inequality between domestic and foreign pre-tax nominal yields and between pre-tax real yields as well. If t_d is greater than t_f, then:

$$i > i^* + \dot{S} \qquad \text{(nominal)} \qquad [10]$$

$$\text{and} \quad (i - \dot{P}) > (i^* - \dot{P}^*) \qquad \text{(real)} \qquad [11]$$

These inequalities suggest one reason why Canadian tax policy—primarily through the FAPI rules—attempts to ensure that domestic and foreign-source interest income of Canadians are taxed equally. In the absence of such equality, if domestic investors are effectively taxed at a lower rate on offshore investment, domestic capital is less than it would otherwise be and domestic real interest rates are higher.

Assume for the moment that Canadian policy to maintain such tax equality is *not* effective, a reasonable first approximation given the numerous opportunities for creative tax accounting for offshore investments. Canadian capital that is shifted offshore would cause the Canadian pre-tax real rate of interest to exceed the pre-tax real rate abroad. Alternatively, the Canadian dollar would depreciate too rapidly to bring [10] into equality. However, if *foreign* countries are able to maintain equal tax rates on domestic and foreign-source income of *their* citizens, then investors from abroad would notice the higher pre-tax yield available in Canada and they would invest in Canada. That action would, in turn, exert downward pressure on Canadian real interest rates and/or increase the rate of appreciation of the Canadian dollar (or stem its rate of depreciation). These effects of increased foreign investment in Canada would restore [10] and [11] to equality. Consequently, the net effect of a Canadian tax differential on domestic versus foreign interest income of Canadians would be to alter the international mix of investment; Canadians would hold more foreign securities while foreigners would invest more in Canada.[36] Canadian investors and investors abroad would be observed to make simultaneous purchases of securities from each other's country, an "abnormal" international capital flow similar to cases discussed in Chapter 7.

An additional degree of complexity may be added to the above scenario. As before, assume that income earned on Canadian investment abroad is taxed at a rate which is lower than the rate on investment income earned in Canada. Furthermore, assume also that Canada—or the interaction of Canadian and foreign tax law—effectively taxes the interest income of foreign holders of Canadian securities at a higher rate than the rate applying to domestic investment in the foreign country. In the past, Canada has in effect brought about this situation through a withholding tax levied on interest paid abroad. Canadian investors, in this case, face lower taxes abroad than in Canada, while foreign investors face relatively higher taxes on Canadian investments than they do on their own domestic investments. The latter differential precludes arbitrage of the non-neutrality created by the former differential. The end result is a persistently higher pre-tax real return on capital in Canada associated with a reduced domestic stock of capital. Brean (1984b) presents evidence of distortions of this type prior to 1975 when Canada imposed a withholding tax on interest paid on long-term corporate bonds held abroad.

Taxes, Inflation, and International Capital Flows

In an internationally integrated capital market, the nominal rate of interest in one country is linked to that in others via exchange rates. However, exchange rate adjustments do not necessarily ensure that relative real rates of interest are not disturbed. Differential rates of inflation interacting with taxation of nominal interest income potentially give rise to distortions of real returns and hence to international reallocations of capital (Hartman 1979, Howard and Johnson 1982).

Internationally mobile capital responding to arbitrage opportunities ensures that investors earn the same expected real after-tax rate of return on domestic investments as on foreign investments. The difference between domestic and foreign investments is essentially that foreign exchange gains and losses (S) enter the calculation of tax on foreign investments whereas, of course, such gains and losses do not enter the yield on domestic investments. Domestic inflation reduces the after-tax yield of both domestic and foreign investments. These considerations are the key to understanding the various possible effects of an increase in one country's inflation rate on domestic and foreign real after-tax yields and on the direction of inflation/tax induced capital flows.

Consider what happens to the various real after-tax returns as a result of a small change in the rate of inflation in the Home country. Domestic investment in the inflating country suffers the burden of the "inflation tax" on nominal yields since the inflation component of yield is taxed. Offshore investments for investors either at home or abroad are inevitably determined in part by the rate of change of the exchange rate. Since Home's inflation causes its currency to depreciate, the foreign exchange effect adds to the return earned by Home investors placing capital abroad while it reduces the return to Foreign investors who place their money in Home. Clearly, for Foreign investors placing capital in the inflating country, the effect of offshore inflation on nominal yields is relevant, just as it is for domestic investors at Home.

Differential effects of inflation on yields of domestic versus foreign investments for Home and Foreign investors hinge on the effects of Home inflation on the Home nominal interest rate and on the rate of change of the exchange rate. In general, investors in a relative low-inflating country who place capital in a relatively high-inflating country receive higher nominal interest payments in a depreciating currency. On the other hand, investors in an inflating country who place capital where the price level is steadier than their own receive lower nominal interest payments in an appreciating currency.

The important question is whether inflation adds point-for-point to the nominal interest rate or the nominal interest rate increases by more than the inflation rate—by a factor of $1 / (1 - t)$—to account for the fact that the inflation component is taxed. We continue to assume that the rate of change of the exchange rate equals the difference between expected rates of inflation.

In a closed economy, the basic Fisher relation—where inflation adds point-for-point to the interest rate—is modified for taxation because investors bear an extra burden of tax since the inflationary component is taxed. This closed economy relation extends to investments placed offshore if domestic and foreign earnings are subject to the same effective rate of tax. Domestic inflation affects the real after-tax yield on domestic and offshore investments equally because the nominal domestic interest rate and the foreign interest rate *plus* the foreign exchange gain or loss are equal and, as we assume, all revenue units are taxed equally. Each point of domestic inflation gives rise to offsetting depreciation of the domestic currency. Investors in the inflating country thus have no incentive to adjust their domestic/foreign mix of investments. They simply bear more tax on both.

Investors offshore similarly are neither drawn to nor discouraged from investment in the inflating country. Their investments in the inflating country earn higher nominal interest which is exactly offset by currency depreciation.

Under the assumptions of the modified Fisher adjustment, the nominal interest rate in the inflating country rises by a factor of $1 / (1 - t)$, that is, by more than point-for-point with inflation. Consequently, investors in the inflating country incur no reduction in real after-tax domestic yields. On the other hand, with respect to capital placed abroad by investors in the inflating country, the impact of inflation on the after-tax real yield is no different in the modified Fisher than in the basic Fisher case. Foreign investment bears an incremental tax, the international variant of the "inflation" tax. Together the effects of inflation serve to encourage domestic investors to leave their capital at home and/or to repatriate capital currently placed abroad. The incentive to reallocate capital arises because the rate of appreciation of the foreign currency—an integral part of the yield on foreign investment—is *less* than the increase in the domestic nominal interest rate.

Investors abroad are likewise encouraged to invest in the inflating country. From their perspective, the mirror image of the preceding case, the currency in which foreign-denominated assets are held depreciates at a rate which is more than compensated by higher nominal interest payments.

In short, if inflation adds more than point-for-point to the nominal interest rate, capital will flow to the country experiencing inflation. The inflow of capital reduces real interest rates and, hence, reduces nominal interest rates as well. This, in turn, reduces both domestic inflation and the rate of depreciation of the currency. Capital inflows subside and a new international financial equilibrium is restored.[37]

Summary

If inflation adds point-for-point to the nominal interest rate, then taxation of nominal interest imposes an "inflation tax" on both domestic and offshore investments of residents of the inflating country. Under conventional assumptions concerning exchange rate adjustment, investors abroad will be hedged from the effects of inflation on the real after-tax yields on their assets in the inflating country.

However, if inflation adds more than point-for-point to the nominal rate of interest, international capital reallocation is induced. A country increasing its inflation rate will increase its capital stock by encouraging its investors to keep capital at home and to repatriate capital placed abroad; foreign investors are likewise encouraged to invest in the inflating country.

Differential taxation of domestic and foreign-source interest earnings tends to reinforce the international capital allocative effects if domestic interest enjoys preferential rates—as was the case when the United States imposed the Interest Equalization Tax on foreign-source interest. An additional reinforcing factor would be non-creditable withholding taxes levied on interest paid abroad. On the other hand, if offshore investment receives preferential treatment, either explicitly by law or implicitly through creative international tax accounting, the flow of repatriated capital to the inflating country would be reduced.

Finally, the underpinning of the modified Fisher adjustment is the demand for bonds by the marginal purchaser of securities denominated in nominal terms. The foregoing analysis points to a potentially serious flaw in the analytic structure of international capital and exchange rate economics. A questionable assumption found in much empirical work is that the relevant tax rate in determining market interest rates is the tax rate imposed by the country issuing bonds. However, since the marginal purchaser of bonds issued by a small open country may well prove to be a foreign investor, the tax rate applied to that investor—usually a tax rate of another country—may have a significant bearing on the size of the domestic interest rate adjustment and, beyond that, on the real interest rate and the exchange rate as well. At present, the theory of international trade and international finance does not satisfactorily integrate the two fundamental axioms of open economy equilibrium—Purchasing Power Parity (for goods markets) and Fisher Open Parity (for capital markets). There is no model which has yet demonstrated that, in the presence of taxation, Purchasing Power Parity and Fisher Open Parity are consistent and that they may hold simultaneously.

9.

Conclusion

A Dozen Key Points

The purpose of this monograph has been to develop a general framework for understanding the effects of taxing capital in an open economy and, within this context, to investigate specific issues in the international dimension of tax policy. An important underlying theme is the economic integration of nations through finance with emphasis on the effects of taxation of interest on internationally mobile capital. The main economic, institutional, and policy points developed in the monograph are:

1. International portfolio investment is the most rapidly growing dimension of the economic integration of nations.

2. International portfolio investment represents the financial counterflow of large external (trade) imbalances among industrial nations. Nations that consume more than they earn (or invest more than they save) must import capital from nations that earn more than they consume (or save more than they invest).

3. While international trade imbalances drive the growth of portfolio investment, the increasing technical sophistication

of international bond markets, including a highly efficient global communications network, facilitates this ever-increasing volume of cross-border capital flows.

4. Internationally mobile capital can be delivered at the speed of light. Through intense competition in international bond markets, bid-ask spreads are reduced to a few basis points, small fractions of one percent. A substantial amount of mobile capital is anonymous, fungible, and easily channeled to taxless investments. These factors result in an untaxed "world interest rate", a benchmark for all portfolio investments. From the perspective of an individual country, both the supply of and demand for internationally mobile capital are highly elastic at the world rate of interest.

5. Because of the high sensitivity of capital movements to the after-tax rate of return, interest income on internationally mobile capital is generally an elusive and, indeed, an ill-advised base for taxation.

6. A nation that taxes interest paid on capital owned by foreigners will have less capital and higher domestic interest rates than if that country did not tax mobile capital.

7. There is a symmetry between taxes on trade (tariffs) and taxes on internationally mobile capital. In both cases taxation distorts the allocation of production, creates economic losses due to inefficiency, and redistributes income.

8. As taxes on trade (tariffs) are eliminated through the GATT and by expansion of trading blocs, taxes on capital shall emerge as relatively more significant in international economic policy.

9. There are self-serving strategic tax policies in the international dimension. For example, a *large* capital-importing nation that levies a tax on interest paid on imported capital potentially can reduce the world rate of interest and thus shift the terms of international financial exchange in its favour. This raises the prospect of an "optimal" tax on interest paid to foreigners. Such possibilities depend crucially on a degree of international capital market segmentation and

thus a less-than-perfectly-elastic foreign demand for a country's capital.

10. A nation that taxes foreign-source interest income of its residents at an effective rate that is higher (lower) than domestic-source interest income in effect establishes a barrier (subsidy) to the export of capital.

11. Canadian taxation of foreign-source income from portfolio investment is intended primarily to constrain opportunities to park income and capital in tax havens. Foreign-source interest income of individuals and financial institutions, in particular off-shore branches of banks, is taxed in Canada on a current basis with credit for foreign taxes paid.

12. Canadian taxation of interest paid to foreign investors, which is essentially restricted to interest on short-term corporate issues, represents a balance between a revenue objective and an efficiency objective.

The following remarks deal with recent policy developments in Canada and abroad that further illustrate the implications of international portfolio capital for domestic policy and national economic performance.

The Role of Exchange Rates

In January 1990, the Bank of Canada modestly relaxed the reins on the domestic money supply following an extended period of tight money, high interest rates and a rising exchange rate. At virtually the same time, and apparently unforeseen by the Bank, interest rates were rising abroad, especially in Germany and Japan. The Canadian movement against the trend in world interest rates caused the Canadian dollar to quickly lose almost four cents on its external value, from more than US$0.865 to US$0.827. The Bank of Canada promptly intervened with massive purchases of Canadian dollars in the foreign exchange markets in order to stem the fall of the dollar. Corresponding action in the Treasury bill auction pushed up short term yields. Within weeks Canadian interest rates, rather than moving lower as planned, rose to their highest levels since the early 1980s. The Canadian dollar remained below US$0.86 until April. By that time the spread between Canadian and US interest rates had widened to 540 basis points. The Governor of the Bank of Canada went on public record saying that the decision to lower interest rates in January was an error in judgment.

During this turbulent time for the Canadian dollar, the Prime Minister made an off the cuff remark about an impending decline in Canadian short term interest rates. In a matter of minutes the Canadian dollar dropped almost one cent on foreign exchange markets—a clear indication of the fact that the demand for Canadian bonds and the external value of the Canadian dollar are determined as much by expectations of future interest rates as by the current level of rates.

The external value of the Canadian dollar experienced above normal volatility in the weeks prior to June 1990 as foreign exchange markets interpreted various signals concerning the probability of acceptance of the Meech Lake Accord on constitutional reform. When the Accord eventually failed to be ratified by the provinces, the Canadian dollar remained remarkably steady, indicating that the outcome of the political wrangling, and in particular the economic implications of continuing constitutional uncertainty, had been discounted in the foreign exchange markets prior to the end of the political process.

These particular examples do not directly involve taxation of international portfolio capital—capital that moves so swiftly and in volumes so large as to cause substantial currency realignment. However, they do illustrate how the fortunes of the dollar are influenced by capital flows that respond to international interest rate differentials along with changes in foreign perceptions of risk. Rapid adjustment in international capital markets follows unanticipated changes in national policy, or mere ruminations about policy.

The exchange rate moves more rapidly than domestic prices. As a result domestic factor costs viewed in international perspective, for example the US-dollar price of Canadian labour relative to US labour, exhibit substantial variance due to exchange rate volatility. Volatility per se is not a serious problem for international economics. Firms involved in trade cope with foreign exchange risk by means of appropriate hedging and diversification strategies. The more serious detriment to trade is exchange rate *misalignment*—sustained departure of the exchange rate from its long-run competitive level. The steady rise in domestic interest rates since 1986, the substantial offshore borrowing and the consequently high Canadian dollar have caused Canadian competitiveness to deteriorate markedly—as much as 30 percent on the basis of international comparisons of production costs. This discourages Canadian exporting and import-substituting industries while prompting shifts of resources to the non-traded goods sectors such as services and construction.

The Tax Policy Dimension

How does taxation relate to these matters? Whither taxation in a world where key relations in the paradigm of international economics seem to have been reversed—from a world where comparative advantage and trade determined the exchange rate with trade imbalances then financed with capital flows, to a world where trade and competitive positions are determined by exchange rates buffeted by speculative international capital flows?

The answers to these questions hinge on the distinction between short-run and long-run influences of the exchange rate on domestic factor costs. It is only in the short-run, that is before domestic and relevant international prices fully adjust to eliminate market imbalances, that flows of portfolio capital create potential trade distortions through effects on the exchange rate. In the longer run, a nation's competitive position is determined by its productive resources and comparative advantage. An important consideration for the long-run is that taxation of international investment can distort the domestic accumulation of capital as well as the international allocation of domestic capital. Thus the international dimension of domestic tax policy adversely affects long-run competitiveness to the extent that taxation restricts the gains associated with a larger and more rapidly growing stock of capital (in the case of restricted capital inflows) or limits nationally beneficial off-shore investments (in the case of restricted capital outflows).

If the exchange rate adjusts without friction to maintain international interest rate parity on an after-tax basis, then international investment flows are always on domestic long-run paths in both capital-importing and capital-exporting nations. In fact, with exchange rate flexibility, the short-run /long-run distinction has no relevance for international portfolio investment. Since international investment responds to international differences in real rates of return due to differences in the productivity of capital and/or national preferences for current consumption, there are no (short-run) capital imbalances so long as exchange rates, as opposed to capital flows, adjust to maintain equal real rates of return. On the other hand, some stickiness in either the exchange rate or domestic prices gives rise to exchange rate misalignment and short-run disequilibria in domestic markets. Domestic goods and factor prices experience momentary changes in their "world" valuations. Since the exchange rate is generally more flexible than domestic prices, domestic financial imbalances—due, for example, to fiscal deficits or monetary contractions—have an immediate impact on the exchange rate as foreign capital flows in to fill the domestic investment-savings gap.

The national gains from efficient international allocation of capital under flexible exchange rates result only if taxation does not otherwise distort investors' decisions.

The International Tax Framework

We have shown in some detail that taxation of international portfolio capital can be analyzed in a framework that is structurally similar to the more familiar framework of trade barriers. Like tariffs on trade, taxation of international portfolio capital creates economic inefficiencies and, again as with trade, the economic cost of these distortions tends to be borne by small nations that must accept world prices. An important theme of our analysis has been to identify the roots of distortion in international investment and to indicate the policy means to capture the economic gains otherwise lost. Whether the focus is on liberalized trading arrangements or on a less restricted investment climate, the point of reference for measuring potential economic gain is the difference between domestic and foreign prices. A nation's economic efficiency is a relative concept that is determined in comparison to the world.

In a closed economy a tax on capital drives a wedge between the marginal return on capital and the rate of return on savings. Capital becomes a relatively more costly factor of production, less capital is employed, and its marginal productivity is higher than if capital was not taxed. In an open economy, two additional distortions arise from capital taxation. First, with respect to savings, taxation is responsible for international differences among savings rates, implying an inefficient allocation of savings across nations and, second, taxation of internationally mobile capital results in differences in the marginal productivity of capital. This implies that world investment is not efficiently allocated across countries.

The concept of the international tax wedge arose when we addressed the economic consequences of taxing portfolio capital. The tax wedge is a static concept. The dynamics of financial adjustment to tax changes are generally more complex but equally relevant for policy. **Changes** in the difference between domestic after-tax yields and foreign yields are followed by rapid and often substantial international capital flows to restore financial equilibrium, regardless of whether the change arises from tax policy, monetary policy, or a real economic disturbance. The following examples illustrate both real and financial responses to recent changes in taxation of portfolio capital.

Learning by Example

In 1984 the United States removed a 30 percent withholding tax on interest paid to foreigners (if the interest income was not effectively connected with the conduct of a trade or business by the taxpayer within the United States). The immediate result was to provide US corporate borrowers with direct access to the Eurobond markets. Previously American borrowers took a circuitous route to the Euromarkets through tax havens such as the Netherlands Antilles. The route through the Caribbean eliminated the US tax liability and, equally important, it did so without identification of the Euro-lenders. In fact, although numerous categories of interest income had been fully or partially exempt from the US withholding tax prior to 1984, relief invariably required identification of the foreign lender. The disclosure requirement discouraged direct American access to the mainstay of the Euromarkets—the anonymous bearer bond. Hence a strategic role emerged for the Netherlands Antilles.

The Netherlands Antilles has no disclosure requirements. Furthermore this Dutch colony conveniently enjoyed the zero withholding tax rate in the motherland's tax treaty with the United States. Thus US financial subsidiaries in the Antilles were able to serve as conduits for Americans to the Euromarkets. Funds from bearer bonds issued abroad simply passed through the Netherlands Antilles en route to America. In turn, interest paid by US corporations to the Euro-bondholders flowed tax free from the US back through the Antilles. The significance of those tiny islands for US corporate tax planning was remarkable. In 1983, the last full year for which the withholding tax was in effect, more than one-third of all interest paid by US borrowers to foreign lenders was paid to addresses in the Netherlands Antilles.

It became obvious to the US tax authorities that the withholding tax generated very little tax revenue since it was easily avoided by taking the route through the Caribbean. The Deficit Reduction Act of 1984 rescinded the tax. A before-and-after comparison is telling. Securities transactions booked within the United States rose almost three-fold, from net $19 billion in 1983 to $50 billion in 1985.

The American experience with withholding taxes on interest paid to foreigners highlights innovative financial arrangements to escape the tax. Since the tax was for all practical purposes avoidable, its economic effects, for example, on foreign investment in the US or on US interest rates, were minimal. In contrast, when Canada removed a withholding tax on interest paid to foreigners, as discussed in Chapter 3, substantial economic distortions were rectified. The Canadian tax had real bite. It was not easily avoided by Canadian firms and, from the foreign bondholders' perspective, it was not fully off-set by foreign tax credits. When the tax was removed, Canadian corporate bonds issued abroad increased substantially. The resulting lower Canadian capital costs and increased foreign investment illustrate the types of economic effects of changing the structure of tax on international investment described throughout this monograph.

The Canadian withholding tax was rescinded only for interest paid on corporate issues with maturity greater than five years. The tax continues to be assessed on interest paid on shorter term issues and, as a result, the Canadian market for short-term corporate paper is effectively segmented from the rest of the world. It is well recognized in the financial community that, for example, the development of Canadian money markets has been slow to mature, the markets lack both breadth (diversity of instruments) and depth (volume), and they are dominated by domestic inter-bank transactions.

Europe in recent years, especially as 1992 approaches, has become a veritable laboratory of experiments in international taxation. Germany, as we have noted, introduced a withholding tax on interest paid to foreigners which was then promptly removed when massive amounts of capital in German financial institutions flowed to the safe havens of Luxembourg and the Netherlands. Belgium, in a classic case of fiscal pathology, managed to reduce its rate of domestic savings while driving up domestic interest rates and forcing financial intermediation to go outside the country. The source of these problems was a punitive 25 percent withholding tax, the "precompte mobilier", that Belgium levied on domestic savings accounts. Foreigners with savings in Belgium were exempt. In effect Belgium extended a tax preference to foreign investors vis-à-vis domestic savers. The precompte mobilier was reduced to 10 percent in February 1990 and, as a result, Belgian domestic savings increased sharply. Fewer Belgians now ride the "Coupon Express" to Luxembourg.

European countries traditionally have imposed a wide variety of restrictions and taxes on international financial trans-actions, most with the clear intent of limiting capital outflows. Policies have taken various forms. Some countries, for example France after 1981 and the United Kingdom until 1979, imposed explicit quotas on foreign investment by residents. Italy until recently levied prohibitive taxes on virtually every foreign financial transaction. Belgium and Luxembourg maintain dual exchange rates to limit capital outflows wherein international financial transactions are conducted at less advantageous terms compared transactions in trade. France, Italy, and Denmark have both quantitative and fiscal restrictions on foreigners' borrowing in domestic capital markets. The effect of such restrictions is to discourage active arbitrage between domestic and international financial markets and to reduce the linkage between domestic and foreign interest rates.

The current direction of policy in Europe, of course, involves considerable change from the past. The European agenda is set to complete the internal market for traded goods and mobile factors of production. This requires removal of internal barriers and harmonization of national policies that could otherwise restrict the free internal flow of goods or factors. With respect to foreign investment, the member nations of the European Community agreed in 1986 to remove capital controls directly related to trade and investment, and in 1988 they agreed to remove all remaining controls. At present the United Kingdom, Germany, the Netherlands, and Denmark have fully eliminated capital controls. Belgium, Luxembourg, France, and Italy still have a few remaining barriers, but these are scheduled to be dismantled soon. The consensus in Europe is that a properly functioning internal market for capital requires a common, and a commonly low, rate of withholding tax on interest paid on foreign portfolio capital.

We have shown that Canada, as much as any nation in the modern world, also must pay careful and constant attention to the international dimension of tax policy. The accelerating economic and financial integration of the world creates new challenges for policy.

The Process of Policy Development

The process to develop appropriate tax policy with respect to international portfolio investment has three components. The process must begin with a clear understanding of the effects—at least in principle—of existing tax arrangements. Next, it is imperative to have a similarly clear idea of policy objectives with an understanding of the potential trade-offs among national objectives. And the third, it is crucial to have evidence on the empirical magnitudes involved and their sensitivity to policy changes. Each of these key ingredients is to some extent lacking in Canada today. Our preliminary survey of the economics of international investment and the influences of taxation raises several questions that would seem to repay further research.

In the first place, it is not possible to design "better" international tax arrangements without an explicit account of the objectives of policy. Further exploration of the aims of current Canadian policy is therefore in order, as is informed discussion of the validity and acceptability of those aims. In particular, both the "neutrality" and "equity" aspects of international taxation require further consideration—the former because of the obvious incompatibility of capital-export neutrality and national welfare maximization and the latter because of the lack of any clear standards for inter-country sharing.[38]

Secondly, even if the objectives of national policy are more clearly specified, the objectives are not easy to attain in the presence of widely varying foreign tax systems. Either a deliberately non-uniform policy must be followed in recognition of the fact that some features of domestic tax law produce different results in conjunction with the systems of other countries. For example, withholding taxes on interest paid to foreigners have different degrees of relief among various residence countries. In international tax policy, as has long been the case in domestic tax policy, uniformity and simplicity is pursued at some expense of efficiency and equity. This trade-off fortunately will fade as increasingly large blocs of countries, such as the European Community, strive to harmonize their domestic tax systems and thus reduce the differences that any one country faces in its collection of neighbours. Canada will benefit from harmonization in Europe in that, for the most part, the relevant external investment community will consist of the United States and one Europe. Nevertheless, both the limits of tolerable non-uniformity set by the "international rules of the game"—the means by which such non-uniformity can be achieved therefore need to be examined closely.[39]

Thirdly, as mentioned at various points in this study, many key parameters critical to the proper design of policy require close empirical examination—including the elasticity of international capital supply, the degree of financial market segmentation, and the interaction of inflation, interest rates, and exchange rates. In the absence of better and more reliable information on such factors, it may be hard to measure the effects on current or proposed policy. In fact it may not be enough merely to refine current policy; many long-standing principles and policies of international

taxation have become outmoded to the point that they are neither
conceptually appropriate nor practicable in the modern international financial world (Bird, 1988). Above all, nations are
beginning to learn that the residence principle is increasingly
difficult to enforce. The obvious alternative is greater reliance on
the source principle (Brean, 1991). In this regard, our analysis of
interest and dividend withholding taxes suggests that the high
priority policy objectives in international taxation—minimal distortion of international investment and equity in the allocation of
tax revenue—could most reasonably be approached through a
multilateral agreement on a common, comprehensive, and low
withholding tax. Otherwise, the forces of international tax arbitrage by investors and tax competition among countries inevitably
will drive the effective rate of tax on internationally mobile capital
to zero.

Similarly, if Canada is genuinely intent on achieving capital-
export neutrality, the validity of the current exemption of foreign-
source "active business income" is questionable (although practical alternatives may not be easy to find). Active business income
is easily disguised as foreign portfolio income which, thus rendered
untaxed by Canada, is *de facto* treated preferentially vis-à-vis
domestic investment. This is much like the Belgian case. The
policy sense and practical significance of both the FAPI system and
Canada's extensive treaty network need closer examination in
light of both Canada's policy aims and the international environment in which policy makers must operate.

We have shown that internal and international tax questions
are ultimately intertwined in modern open economies. If countries
cannot successfully and equitably tax international income, they
are unlikely to be able to tax domestic capital income successfully
either, given the ease with which international capital flows to the
source of highest after-tax return.

Indeed, many aspects of domestic tax policy, involving equity
as well as efficiency, are subject to strong international influences.
Since a country that cannot effectively tax capital income cannot
for long maintain an acceptable progressive income tax, what is at
stake in the international dimension of taxation is not a minor
matter, of interest only to specialist tax practitioners and a few
academic economists, but rather it is an issue that, in the end, may
well determine the future of the income tax itself in the increas-

ingly integrated modern world. As a result of the openness of the Canadian economy, the taxation of international portfolio investment poses an especially crucial set of issues for Canadian economic policy.

Notes

1. In contrast, foreign *direct* investment refers to equity capital as part of a larger package of technology, management, and business arrangements. It entails control of local enterprise whereas portfolio investment does not—although this line is often difficult to draw in theory and is invariably arbitrary in practice. Foreign direct investment is carried out by corporations pursuing profit and growth opportunities abroad. Corporations establish foreign subsidiary operations instead of, say, exporting or licensing, for many different reasons, depending on the particular circumstances of the specific investment. For further discussion of the taxation of foreign direct investment, see Brean (1984a), especially Chapters 7 and 8.

2. The sum of domestic and foreign-owned capital meets the total domestic capital requirement. However, while domestic and foreign-owned capital are substitutes, they are not *perfect* substitutes. Without some fundamental domestic preference for domestic investment, or a fundamental aversion to foreign investment, however small, no equilibrium domestic/foreign mix of capital could be specified. In effect, it is implicitly always assumed that, if other things are exactly equal, domestic investors invest at home.

3. It is important to bear in mind potential inconsistencies between the flow data in Table 1, derived from the Capital Account of the Balance of Payments, and the stock statistics of Table 2 which have been constructed by Statistics Canada from a different perspective and using additional data sources. For example, Table 1 reports a continuous outflow of net direct investment from Canada since 1975, whereas Table 2 shows a continuous rise in the stock of foreign direct investment in Canada through the same period. The dramatic difference is explained by the fact that the flow data reflect strictly international financial flows that pass through the Capital Account and thus do not capture important increments to the stock of foreign firms that is financed through borrowing in Canada. The stock data in Table 2 capture these latter phenomena.

   Fortunately, for our purposes, discrepancies between stocks and accumulated net flows are less of an empirical problem for portfolio investment which essentially all flows through the Capital Account of the Balance of Payments. For example, the cumulative net portfolio flow from 1970 to 1984 as reported in Table 1 is $87 billion while the change in the stock of portfolio capital as calculated from Table 2 for the same period is $88 billion.

4. For depreciation to provide effective stimulus to output and employment, the increased demand for exports must be met at prevailing (pre-depreciation) domestic prices. If producers raise prices in terms of domestic currency in order to maintain the real world price, the effects of depreciation are neutralized. Real effects are dissipated in domestic inflation. Exchange rate declines only provide economic stimulus by raising product prices relative to wages—that is, by reducing real wages. The reluctance of governments to let this unpleasant result ensue is one reason why devaluation is often not an effective stimulus to exports.

5. The relationships between interest rates, capital flows and exchange rates are fundamental to understanding the high value of the United States dollar until mid 1987 and its implications for trade. The United States policy mix was essentially easy fiscal and tight monetary policy. The latter kept United States interest rates high and thus attracted foreign capital. These capital inflows required foreign exchange transactions entailing buying pressure on the

United States dollar which kept the value of the dollar high. Effects on the world economy—involving the United States trade imbalance—followed from this distortion of the United States exchange rate.

6. This is a central point in Jenkins and Deutsch (1982).

7. The following points are developed by Brean (1984b) in the context of an empirical study of the effects of the removal of the Canadian withholding tax on interest paid to foreign bondholders. The results of that study indicate that after the tax was removed the cost of capital to Canadian corporations fell significantly and the volume of portfolio flows to the Canadian corporate sector rose substantially.

8. More complete analysis of the return on fixed capital would also take explicit account of the marginal excess burden imposed on the economy due to the distortion of the tax, but this theme cannot be pursued here.

9. As one reviewer of an earlier draft observed, it is true that Canada nominally has a per country method for calculating foreign tax credits. However, at least in the case of foreign direct investments, it is relatively simple to achieve overall limitation treatment by holding subsidiaries and other investments through a foreign holding company. This allows foreign taxes from many jurisdictions to be aggregated in the underlying foreign tax account of the holding company affiliate. The same effect may sometimes be achieved by holding foreign investments through a foreign branch where it can be shown that the investments are held in the course of carrying on a business at that branch.

10. For further discussion of different systems, see Sato and Bird (1975).

11. For example, the United Kingdom extends such a credit to certain United States investors.

12. The present Canadian dividend credit has recently been severely criticized by Jenkins (1986) for many valid reasons. His proposed solution of a compensatory tax similar to the British Advance Corporation Tax (ACT) would, however, violate the neutrality criterion. Fur further discussion of this issue, see Bird (1987b).

13. As before, it is assumed the corporation tax is not shifted. If universal shifting of the corporation tax is assumed, the exemption of foreign income may be justified on national efficiency grounds, as in the world efficiency case: see Sato and Bird (1975).

14. Moreover, in the case of direct investment, the *current* taxation of subsidiary income would still be required, because the deferral of taxation on reinvested foreign income would otherwise, from the standpoint of national efficiency, unduly encourage foreign investment. The failure to tax such income currently (of course, with deduction of foreign corporate tax) would encourage capital outflows beyond the point where the net (after-foreign-tax) profits equal the gross domestic profits and would therefore result in national losses. But as shown in Sato and Bird (1975), current taxation obviously involves substantial difficulties if either Canada or the capital-importing country adopts some form of integration.

15. This section of the purpose and structure of the international tax treaty network abridges Brean (1984a), pages 10-15.

16. For further discussion of principles, problems, and policies, see Peggy B. Musgrave (1972) and Musgrave and Musgrave (1972).

17. To some extent this result has been codified in the model tax treaty prepared by the Organization for Economic Cooperation and Development (OECD, 1977), although the United States has developed its own similar but not identical model (Rosenbloom, 1985).

18. These differences are recognized in the model treaty set out by the United Nations (UN 1982), although the influence of the OECD model is still very strong.

19. See Burge and Brown (1979).

20. This section is based closely on Brean (1984a), Chapter 9. See also Perry (1984), Chapter 8. More detailed discussions may be found in Dancy et al. (1982) and Harris (1981).

21. Booth (1987) analyzes this issue in detail. He demonstrates that the potential effect of the Canadian dividend tax credit (for Canadians only) on the domestic/foreign mix of equity ownership varies across industrial sectors. The effect

depends on certain corporate characteristics such as dividend yield and risk. Mutti and Grubert (1985) also explore the importance of a difference in resident versus non-resident tax treatment. More fundamentally, Mutti and Grubert demonstrate how international capital mobility alters the incidence and capital formation incentive of domestic taxes on capital incomes. Only a modest degree of international capital mobility is necessary to substantially alter closed-economy patterns of tax incidence.

22. A corporation operating abroad in the form of a branch is taxed as if operating in Canada, that is, on an accrual basis with a (limited) foreign tax credit. It is not entirely clear from any point of view why a 100 percent owned subsidiary (let alone one 51 percent owned) should be taxed differentially but the present system of taxing subsidiaries is, as described in the text, totally different.

23. The equity percentage of a Canadian shareholder of a non-resident corporation for the purpose of these rules includes two factors: *direct* equity percentage and *indirect* investments. The direct equity percentage is the highest percentage of any of the claims of outstanding stock held by the Canadian shareholder. However, if that same shareholder also has an interest in the foreign affiliate through another corporation, for example an offshore financial holding company, the direct and indirect interest are combined to produce the total equity percentage.

24. An obvious way to avoid FAPI treatment is to keep below the 10 percent equity rule as has been done recently in some offshore mutual fund operations in tax haven countries.

25. Capital gains derived on the sale of assets used in connection with active business abroad are also excluded from FAPI.

26. See Dancy et al., Chapter 18, for detailed examples.

27. Actually, "scheduled countries" would be a more accurate term: in 1982, 51 countries qualified for this treatment, ranging from Antigua to Zambia. The original idea behind this distinction appears to have been that "treaty" countries had tax rates and structures similar to Canada but it is impossible to believe this is the case with the present very diverse set of treaty countries.

28. Indeed many serious complexities—stacking rules, base determination rules, treatment of reorganizations, et cetera —have been omitted in this simplified discussion.

29. For a detailed discussion of United States policy in this area, see Gordon (1981). For a more general discussion, see Arnold (1986) as well as the recent treatment in OECD (1987).

30. For an attempt at analyzing the United States provision intended to achieve similar results, see Hufbauer and Foster (1976).

31. For further discussion of such developments in their historical context, see Brean (1987).

32. The issues in this section receive more extensive treatment in Brean (1984a) Chapter 6.

33. A tax on foreign exchange transactions has been suggested by Tobin (1978) and Dornbusch (1986) for a somewhat different reason than the present concern for small-country interest rate independence. Tobin and Dornbusch recommend the tax to countries concerned about exchange rate instability and the consequences of trade. The view is that exchange rates are "excessively efficient" (Tobin), that capital sloshes back and forth in response to trivial disturbances, and that a tax on foreign exchange transactions would reduce exchange rate variability by reducing the extent to which speculators could react to small changes in the attractiveness of different countries' assets. The key question in this case is whether investor expectations, the force underlying the pattern of exchange rate movements, are destabilizing if left to themselves. For some evidence that they are destabilizing, see Frankel and Meese (1987).

34. For an analysis of the price Canada paid in terms of monetary independence for this exemption, see Grady (1977).

35. To reiterate a point stressed in Chapter 2, the link between international flows of financial capital and factor capital is tenuous. Much of the ebb and flow of financial capital involves reallocation of ownership and foreign indebtedness rather than shifts of factor capital.

36. Note that this effect would to some extent be offset, as noted in Chapter 4, by the operation of the present dividend tax

credit system in Canada, which tends to induce the opposite
shift in the ownership mix of equities.

37. Hartman (1979) shows the conditions under which inflation
induces capital to flow to the inflating country. Howard and
Johnson (1982) show in greater detail how inflation reduces
the real interest rate in the inflating country. At the same
time, inflation reduces the effective rate of tax on foreign
investment income in the inflating country. Hansson and
Stuart (1986) demonstrate that the frequently observed
empirical finding that inflation in an open economy adds
roughly point-for-point to the nominal interest rate is an
equilibrium result due to international financial arbitrage
under specific assumptions, including purchasing power
parity and equal taxation of domestic and foreign source
income (including foreign exchange gains and losses).

Hartman and Howard and Johnson both describe
unsustainable disequilibria—either continuous capital flows
or a persistent international differential in real interest rats.
Hansson and Stuart, on the other hand, describe an
equilibrium result without an adjustment mechanism. These
three positions—each correct in its own right—are complementary in the sense that disequilibria represent the
transition to new equilibria. Inflation reduces the effective
rate of tax on foreign investment, which is followed by capital
inflows, reduced interest rates and lower inflation and,
eventually, a new equilibrium in which the domestic Fisher
relation holds. Mishkin's (1984) substantial evidence that in
several small open economies (France, West Germany,
Netherlands, Switzerland) inflation is highly correlated—
that is, moves concurrently with—the real interest rate is
also consistent with this interpretation of sequential events.

38. The latter issue has been raised particularly sharply recently
in connection with the "unitary tax" discussion and the
consequent international wrangle as to who has the "right" to
tax what share of corporate income; see Bird and Brean
(1986).

39. See Bird (1987A and b) for such discussion in the specific
cases of Australia and New Zealand.

References

Arnold, Brian J. (1986), *The Taxation of Controlled Foreign Corporations: An International Comparison*, Toronto: Canadian Tax Foundation.

Bird, Richard M. (1988), "Shaping a New International Tax Order," *Bulletin for International Fiscal Documentation*, June.

_____ (1987a), "International Aspects of Tax Reform in Australia," in *Australian Tax Reform in Retrospect and Prospect*, J.G. Head, ed.; Sydney: Australian Tax Research Foundation.

_____ (1987b), *The Taxation of International Income Flows: Issues and Approaches*, Wellington: Institute for Policy Studies.

_____ (1987c), "The Public Sector in Canada: An Overview," in *Issues in Public Sector Analysis*, Balbir Sahni, ed.; Ottawa: Shastri Indo-Canadian Institute, pp. 1-56.

Bird, Richard M. and Donald J.S. Brean (1986), "The Interjurisdictional Allocation of Income and the Unitary Tax Debate," *Canadian Tax Journal* 34(6), November-December, pp. 1377-1416.

111

_____ (1985), "Canada/United States Tax Relations: Issues and Perspectives," in *Canada/United States Trade and Investment Frictions*, Deborah Fretz, Robert Stern and John Whalley, eds.; Toronto: Ontario Economic Council, pp. 391-425.

Booth, Laurence D. (1987), "The Dividend Tax Credit and Canadian Ownership Objectives," *Canadian Journal of Economics*, 20(2), May, pp. 321-39.

Brean, Donald J.S. (1990), "Here or There? Conflict Between the Source and Residence Principles," in *Taxation to 2000 and Beyond*, Richard M. Bird and J.M. Mintz, eds., Toronto: Canadian Tax Foundation.

_____ (1987), "The International Dimension of Canadian Tax Policy: Contributions of Carter and Subsequent Developments," in *The Royal Commission on Taxation: 20 Years Later*, Neil brooks, ed.; Toronto: Carswell Press.

_____ (1984a), *International Issues in Taxation: The Canadian Perspective*, Toronto: Canadian Tax Foundation.

_____ (1984b), "International Portfolio Capital: The Wedge of the Withholding Tax," *National Tax Journal* 37(2), June.

Burge, Marianne and Robert D. Brown (1979), "Negotiations for a New Tax Treaty Between Canada and the United States—A Long Story," *Canadian Tax Journal* 27, January-February, pp. 94-104.

Burgess, David F. (1985), "On the Relevance of Export Demand Conditions for Capital Income Taxation In Open Economies," Discussion Paper No. 287, Ottawa: Economic Council of Canada.

Dancy, K.J., Friesen, R.A. and Timbrell, D.Y. (1982), *Canadian Taxation of Foreign Affiliates* (3rd ed.): Toronto: CCH Canadian Ltd.

Dixit, Avinash (1985), "Tax Policy in Open Economies," in *Handbook of Public Economics*, A.J. Auerbach and M. Feldstein, Vol. I, Amsterdam: North Holland, pp. 313-7.

Dornbusch, Rudiger (1986), "Flexible Exchange Rates and Excess Capital Mobility," *Brookings Papers on Economic Activity*, 1, pp. 209-26.

Fisher, Irving (1930), *The Theory of Interest*, New York: MacMillan.

Frankel, Jeffery A. and Richard Meese (1987), "Are Exchange Rates Excessively Variable?" in *NBER Macroeconomics Annual 1987*, Stanley Fisher, ed.; Cambridge, Massachusetts: The MIT Press.

Gordon, Richard A. (1981), *Tax Havens and Their Use by United States Taxpayers—An Overview*, A Report to the Commissioner of Internal Revenue, the Assistant Attorney General (Tax Division) and the Assistant Secretary of the Treasury (Tax Policy), Washington, D.C., Internal Revenue Service, 1981.

Goulder, L.H. (1989), "Implications of Introducing U.S. Withholding Taxes on Foreigners' Interest Income," a paper presented to the NBER Conference on Tax Policy and The Economy: Cambridge, Massachusetts, November.

Grady, Patrick (1977), "The Interest Equalization Tax" (unpublished Ph.D. Thesis), University of Toronto.

Hansson, Ingemar and Charles Stuart (1986), "The Fisher Hypothesis and International Capital Markets," *Journal of Political Economy* 94(6), pp. 1130-7.

Harris, Edwin C. (1981), *Canadian Income Taxation*, 2nd ed.; Toronto: Butterworth.

Hartman, David G. (1985), "Tax Policy and Foreign Direct Investment," *Journal of Public Economics* 26, pp. 107-21.

_____ (1979), "Taxation and The Effects of Inflation on the Real Capital Stock in an Open Economy," *International Economic Review* 20(2), June, pp. 417-25.

Howard, David H. and Karen H. Johnson (1982), "Interest Rates, Inflation, and Taxes: The Foreign Connection," *Economics Letters* 9(2), pp. 181-4.

Hufbauer, Gary and D. Foster (1976), "United States Taxation of the Undistributed Income of Control Foreign Corporations," in *Essays in International Taxation*, Washington: United States Department of Treasury.

Jenkins, Glenn P. (1987), "The Role and Economic Implications of the Canadian Dividend Tax Credit," Economic Council of Canada Discussion Paper No. 307, June.

Jenkins, Glenn P. and Antal Deutsch (1982), "Tax Incentives, Revenue Transfers, and the Taxation of Income From Foreign Investment," in *Tax Policy Options in the 1980s*, Wayne R.

Thirsk and John Whalley, eds.; Toronto: Canadian Tax Foundation.

Keynes, J.M. (1924), "Foreign Investment and National Advantage," *The Nation and Anthenaeum* (August 9).

Levi, Maurice D. (1977), "Taxation and 'Abnormal' International Capital Flows," *Journal of Political Economy* 85, June, pp. 635-46.

Mishkin, Frederic S. (1984), "The Real Interest Rate: A Multi-Country Empirical Study," *Canadian Journal of Economics* 27(2), May, pp. 283-311.

Musgrave, Peggy B. (1972), "International Tax Base Division and the Multinational Corporation," *Public Finance* 27(4), pp. 396-413.

_____ (1969), *United States Taxation of Foreign Investment Income*, Cambridge, Massachusetts: Harvard Law School International Tax Program.

Musgrave, Richard A. and P.B. Musgrave (1972), "Inter-Nation Equity," in *Modern Fiscal Issues*, R.M. Bird and J.G. Head; Toronto: University of Toronto Press.

Mutti, John and Harry Grubert (1985), "The Taxation of Capital Income in an Open Economy," *Journal of Public Economics* 27, pp. 291-309.

Organization for Economic Cooperation and Development (1987), *International Tax Avoidance and Evasion*, Paris.

_____ (1977), *Model Double Taxation Convention on Income and Capital*, Paris.

Papke, L.E. (1989), "International Differences in Capital Taxation and Corporate Borrowing Behavior: Evidence From the U.S. Withholding Tax," a paper presented to the NBER Workshop on International Taxation, Cambridge, Massachusetts: August.

Perry, J. Harvey (1984), *Taxation in Canada*, 4th ed.; Toronto: Canadian Tax Foundation.

Rosenbloom, David (1983), "Tax Treaty Abuse: Policies and Issues," *Law and Policy in International Business* 15(3), pp. 763-831.

Sato, Mitsuo and R.M. Bird (1975), "International Aspects of the Taxation of Corporations and Shareholders," *International Monetary Fund Staff Papers* 22, July.

Shoup, Carl S. (1969), *Public Finance*, Chicago: Aldine.

Tobin, James (1978), "A Proposal for International Monetary Reform", *Eastern Economic Journal* 4(3, 4), July/October, pp. 153-9. Reprinted in Tobin, *Essays in Economics*, 1985, Cambridge: MIT Press, pp. 488-94.

Whalley, John (1982), "Discriminatory Features of Domestic Factor Tax Systems in a Goods Mobile-Factors Immobile Trade Model: An Empirical General Equilibrium Approach," *Journal of Political Economy* 88, No. 6.

Other Joint Centre-Institute Publications

Living with Free Trade   1990
Edited by Richard G. Dearden, Michael M. Hart
and Debra P. Steger

A North American Free Trade Agreement: 1990
The Strategic Implications for Canada
by Michael Hart

Due Process and Transparency in   Forthcoming
InternationalTrade Law
Edited by Michael M. Hart and Debra P. Steger

Order address:
The Institute for Research on Public Policy
P.O. Box 3670 South
Halifax, Nova Scotia
B3J 3K6
1-800-565-0659 (toll free)

Related Institute Publications

Order address:
The Institute for Research on Public Policy
P.O. Box 3670 South
Halifax, Nova Scotia B3J 3K6
1-800-565-0659 (toll free)

0520